# INVOLUTION

Stories, Poems and Essays from the first two years of *Line Zero*

# INVOLUTION

Stories, Poems and Essays from the first two years of *Line Zero*

## RENDA BELLE DODGE
## BAILEY SHOEMAKER RICHARDS

### EDITORS

ISBN-13: 978-0615813660
ISBN-10: 0615813666

Book design © Pink Fish Press
Printed in the United States of America
First Edition
10 9 8 7 6 5 4 3 2 1
www.thepinkfishpress.com


Managing Editor
Renda Belle Dodge
renda@linezero.org

Literary Content Editor
Bailey Shoemaker Richards
bailey@linezero.org

Line Zero is published quarterly by Pink Fish Press.
For information on advertising, showering the contributors with gifts, subscribing or
submitting please visit LineZero.org

# CONTENTS

# Contents

INVOLUTION
*The act or an instance of enfolding or entangling*

# INTRODUCTION

*Line Zero is the place where it all starts. It's the blank page, the empty beginning and the start of something new. It's the excitement of a story about to unfold, and it's also the terrifying emptiness of writer's block. Most of all, it's taking that step into artistic creation.*

When we started *Line Zero*, it was in the hopes that we'd be doing something different, something that showcased literature as art right alongside photography and art pieces. We started with an idea and it became so much more. We've had experts and laymen, we've had edgy pieces and traditional poetry. It's been backed by an amazing staff and volunteers.

What struck me the most as we compiled the stories, poems and essays for this collection was the amazing diversity. Everything we have in here is rich and challenging and beautiful. And we couldn't have done it without the lifeblood of *Line Zero*: our extremely talented contributors.

Here, as we delve into the third volume, we can only hope to continue to grow and reach beyond the first line, into the many more that come as we turn inward and entangle our past into the future of this publication—which we have called on many occasions, always affectionately, 'the little lit zine that could'. Thank you so much for being a part of it—readers, artists, supporters and contributors—I love every single one of you.

Renda Belle Dodge
May 2013

# TONIGHT HAS BEEN A NIGHTMARE
### Sarah Lucille Marchant
### Volume 2, Issue 3

quickened footsteps
beat the tears through the sleet
and the snow
on the sidewalk
slick, slippery blacktop

tiny feet
trailing droplets
cursing the stars
stuck
in cold constellations

for rising above
cutting the cords
mocking the world
scorning the captives

# An Open Letter to my Father

Ken Davis
Volume I, Issue 3

Dear Dad,

The muscles surrounding my gut would always tighten when I heard your car coming down the alley behind the house. The crunch of pea gravel being churned by the weight of grandpa's old Ford Falcon would signal your arrival home from work. At the proper angle of rubber to rock, the gravel would catch some air and collide with a pop against the aged gray cedar fence in the back yard. (A good section of which is still there today, blanketed by thin tendrils of lichen rising off the slick, mildew stained wood like clumps of dusty green coral; it's starting to lean into the yard.) I'd be sitting in one of the recliners facing the television and I'd jam the lever forward to lower the foot rest and get out of the chair. I didn't think you'd approve of me watching TV while reading another colorful Travis McGee adventure by John D. MacDonald. If I'd been reading Kipling's *Kim* you might not have minded. But I wasn't going anywhere near that tome. Instead I'd go to the kitchen table, or the living room, and open my school books. I pretended not to notice when you'd come through the back gate, so buried was I in study. You would take those long, pounding strides down the short cement walkway. My peripheral vision would catch your pine tree green, Forest Service uniform and Smokey the Bear hat. I'd put on my deep, scholastic concentration face and only look up when you flung the sliding glass door open so fast I thought it would derail. Your face went well with my apprehension. Uncompromising, as if the paint on the walls colored the dissatisfaction you knew would soon leach through. We wouldn't speak. You'd go upstairs and I'd clear my school books from the table and take them to my room, MacDonald tucked under my arm. This is how my teenage mind saw you.

Understanding comes with age. The mind is a cheeky bastard that spreads lies because it has no idea what truth is. I convicted you of being disappointed with me having no evidence that you ever were. You never raised your voice with me unless I was doing something stupid. We never had cross words. You never belittled me or embarrassed me. There was never any Pat Conroyesque abuse or neglect ala *The Great Santini*. In other words, my childhood was normal. If I had questions, you would answer them. If I needed help with my math, you stopped what you were doing and went over it with me with the utmost patience, even when my brain couldn't comprehend that equation from sixth grade involving 33 1/3$^{rd}$. Reverend Fisher was there that night and even he couldn't help me with it. The problem was mine, not yours.

Strother Martin said it best in *Cool Hand Luke*. "What we've got here is, failure to communicate…" You could have long conversations with your other children. And the topics were wide ranging. You and me? Nothing. True, it was rare that you could speak to your oldest child without some tension, but there was conversation. You loved to fish. I liked baseball. I went fishing with you. You never played catch with me. Resentful? Nope. Never was. Was I jealous of my brother and younger sister with whom there seemed to be a relationship? Far from it. I was relieved because it took the pressure off of me to even try to find a connection. I could go to my room and read, listen to my music, or go ride my bike for hours and just be. Phew!

For whatever reason, you and I avoided each other. You even admitted to one of my sibling's that you and I didn't talk. You can't imagine the relief I felt. I even laughed. It meant that you were as uncomfortable as I was. I can't fault you or make a judgment about it. That's just the way it was.

But let's forget the angst of my teens (such drama) and discuss my post college career: pizza restaurant manager, three locations. All that tuition you paid was wasted. That's how I felt. You never made such a statement, but I wondered.

Once again, my mind was making up crap and I was accepting it as truth. It was during this time that I married Teri and we bought a mortgage. You retired from the Forest Service and then spent several years managing the Mason County fairgrounds. After that, you went back to school to learn the income-tax racket. You opened your own business and ran it out of the house. You volunteered hours of your time helping low income folks who couldn't afford professional tax help. You built a clientele and started to turn a modest profit. But it was never about the money; you did it to help people. I think it was the thrill of finding obscure deductions. Case in point: the Native American with the bulldozer. Your research discovered that since he'd used the dozer in support of Native American fisheries, the income he'd made was tax free. Loop-holes, you liked finding loop-holes that would stick it to The Man. I admired that and I admired the drive you put into such diverse occupations because I was in my mid thirties and couldn't find my passion. Not that I was looking for it.

January through April became Tax Season. You were very busy, but the rest of the year was yours and you took on many hobbies. You practiced your culinary skills. I didn't find out until years later that when you were first considering college courses it was a tossup between Forestry and Culinary. I never would have thought that. But it makes sense. You were a tremendous baker, (your granddaughter still talks about "grandpa's rolls") you took over Thanksgiving and later most of the daily cooking. You took an interest in agriculture and built raised, irrigated garden beds above the useless, rock quarry buried beneath your backyard. You installed a greenhouse for tomatoes and herbs. And in the evenings you started going to a writing group. Driven. Meanwhile I can't fight the onslaught of Morning Glory advancing through my yard, scything every decent vegetable like Sherman's march through the south. I deserted my doomed corn crop when I could no longer distinguish the stalks from the blossoms of that noxious weed. Not so driven.

But your bread. Bread warms any house. Bread takes away all stress. Bread brings people together and gives them something to talk about. In the Bible yeast is always used as a metaphor for corruption. Yeast was the thing that corroded the iron muting our mouths. As soon as I got the bug to bake, you started sending me books on the subject and <u>Cooks Illustrated</u> showed up in my mail box. We started talking about flour, water, yeast, proper gluten formation, oven temperature, brick baking versus pans, and grains. You were always in the wheat camp while I had allied myself with oat. Then came the great flood of sour dough starters, twelve different cultures from various geographical, bread hot spots. Each had their own distinct flavor. The Middle East starters were akin to horse sweat. Out of respect I kept them for years though I secretly prayed for their deaths. Twenty five years later I still have three of the original twelve disciples of wild yeast. The point is… well I suspect you know what the point is. We found common ground and where silence had once born its dead weight around our tongues we could now speak of all things culinary. Sadly, your other son has proven to be challenged in this arena. He tries but has yet to graduate beyond the simple hash cook…well, he does make a good pizza and he's figured out that the Weber and five pounds of Kingsford has more uses than cooking hot dogs. But your daughter's idea of a hot meal involves the toaster. Fresh vegetables mean a can was just opened. She would say that of the two of us she would survive the apocalypse. If survival means canned vegetables then I'm out. I'll spare you any more grief on this subject.

Grief. There's a great segue. When the news of malignancy first came to me I have to say that I was surprised that a family rule had been broken. Amongst the Davis/Fleming clan, disease is never discussed prior to the funeral announcement. It's considered bad luck. I suspect this comes from our strong British heritage. Stiff upper lip and all that. But the cancer never really worried me because I knew that the power that drove you would be there to help you face this setback. I was more worried about Mom. That's why I came down every week for chemo-day. I suspect you knew that and I also suspect you appreciated it, though it was never discussed, that would be bad luck. I prefer to think that it was generally accepted and obvious.

I look back on those weeks with fondness. That sounds awful, I know. But I'm not speaking of the illness or the treatments. I am speaking of the time spent with you and Mom. In truth it was not my idea to make the trips. It was explained to me, in very clear terms by Teri, that I'd better get my ass down to Shelton. She didn't understand the rule, and I thank her for that. My failure to take the initiative in this endeavor, I believe, is due to the fact that I truly wasn't concerned and I didn't think there was anything I could do anyway. Maybe that was just an excuse to avoid the situation; I'll ask Carl Jung if I ever get the chance; Freud would just irritate me.

Being that communication between us was still fairly limited to benign topics, a routine developed that was mutually advantageous. I'd drive down the evening before chemo. In the morning I'd take you and Mom to the hospital. While you went in for treatment, Mom and I would shop for dinner and then we'd come back to pick you up. (My memory tells me that we never did take-out. If we did, I've buried the atrocity deep in my subconscious where I hope it never surfaces. Take-out would be shameful. Take-out is only applicable after long days of house painting or wood splitting. That's it!)

I'm not sure how you felt about somebody else cooking in your kitchen. I think it would bother me. Not because the meal would be inferior, and not because somebody else would be wielding MY chef's knife in THEIR dirty, greasy paws (well, maybe that) but because I wouldn't be the one with busy hands, something I'm sure I inherited from you. Half the fun of cooking is the prep and the two or three beers consumed while this takes place. To your credit you gave me free reign. I didn't take it personal when, after we came back from the hospital, you went to the garage to pour a glass of fine wine from "the box". I knew it wasn't because you had to brace yourself for gastronomic disaster. In fact you paid me the highest compliment as you relaxed in your E-Z chair. Many times you uttered "Oh my, that smells good". Of course garlic, mushrooms and wine deglazing the pan have that effect. And then you'd have to get out of your chair to check things out. You never asked questions, you just let me do it. Thank you.

Over the years it has always impressed me that you never complained about the cancer, at least to me. I don't know whether you said anything to the others, and if you did that's between you and them. I saw you as stoic. I saw no fear in you at all. It was as if you'd accepted whatever was going to happen. I do know that you hated feeling like crap. Who wouldn't? The only thing you ever said to me on the subject was, "This is such a damn nuisance"; an observation on your part, not a grievance.

If I had to guess, I'd say you were pretty pissed that disease interfered with your writing. You were just starting to roll with it. You'd had the story of *Spike the Finch* published in the <u>Mason County Journal</u>. You were home-publishing <u>Succotash</u>, that little booklet of short stories and poetry your writing group put together. You e-mailed me a story called *Rednecks*. I think I told you at the time that I thought it was pretty damn good. Buried deep in your old Mac, I know there's a novel. I've snooped around for it, too. I haven't found it yet but I have discovered plenty of other unfinished pieces.

You may not remember, but I wrote stories in grade school. I'd plagiarized them from the NBC Mystery Movie of the Week and added my own fourth grade twist. They were brilliant. I always liked writing to friends, as well. I would fill them with outrageous stories that were obvious fabrications. I thought they were hilarious. My friends stopped writing back. Rejection. So I don't think it was coincidence that I chose journalism as a major. I liked to write. I just hated writing news. I loved the film shoots and the editing process. I even won best in class for that slide show presentation, complete with music soundtrack, about a frustrated golfer. It never clicked in my thick head that I was focusing on the wrong medium. I was good at telling stories. I was uninspired by journalism.

Cooking with you and for you, reading your stories, these are the things that inspired my own path. To write was not a conscious decision. Little things, like a question on a dry erase board at work, sparked creativity. An irritating two word phrase overused by a co-worker spawned a novel which then begat a trilogy. Now I'm entering the world of pitching to literary agents, query letters and rejection slips. I'm looking at becoming an indie-writer as the daunting literary world seems to be growing ever more archaic. I'm standing in the same place you were before cancer won the battle. And as I write this it occurs to me that this is the only letter I've ever written to you. I'm not going to sit here and say that I should have done it before. I have no use for living in the past. Besides, I like to think that some of my best ideas are coming from you. The reason I know this is that several years after you passed, Teri had a dream. The message given? Finish the book. At the time, all of my writing was clandestine so she thought it had something to do with your work. I knew it didn't. I'd put my writing away. I wasn't going to pick it up again. Teri and I were going through a rough patch and I couldn't find my muse. I put all the shit aside, sat down and focused. I finished. Well, it's never really done, is it? It's gone through multiple revisions and a massive re-write from beginning to end. I think I've taken it as far as I can. I'm ready for the next step. I've found my drive.

How do I say thank you? Maybe I just did. But I want to take it further so I'm submitting *Rednecks* to a literary journal for you and without your permission. You're welcome. What impressed me about this story was your use of brevity to describe such dire circumstances. It's subtle but creepy. It surprised me. So thanks, Dad. We had more in common than I ever thought. I just couldn't see it at the time. Now I do.

Ken

P.S. I finally read Kipling. You were right.

# Rednecks
### John M. Davis

Claude drove his John Deere tractor across a field stippled with corn stobs. The towed disks uprooted the stobs, flipped them over, then sliced them into a barely dampened soil. He saw his neighbor, Ira, standing at the edge of the field, where their properties joined. He turned the tractor in Ira's direction and slightly accelerated. The resonance of the engine played on his ears like an orchestra. At times he imagined hearing hymns on the church organ. He pulled up near Ira and killed the engine. Stepping off the tractor, he swung around, rotated the knots from his shoulders, and looked up at the pale yellow sky.

"Hot for April."

"It's gonna get hotter."

"Seems likely."

"Are you going to plow?"

"Nope, I'm just going to disk, then plant in a trench. If anything sprouts, I'll pull the soil around, then mulch. I'll rake the other fields to reclaim the stubble."

"Where'd you get the seed?"

"I put some seed corn away last fall, and I got hold of some Indian maize. Thought it could maybe take the heat."

"Got any to spare?"

"Dunno, might. We'll see if there's any left after this forty is planted. If not, we'll share what comes off this field."

"You think there's any use?"

"Dunno. Gotta try. Gotta eat and my boy's sending the grandchildren down soon."

"Him and his missus coming?"

"Later."

"The banker givin' you any grief?"

"Nope, he seems preoccupied."

"Wouldn't wonder."

The two old friends looked each other in the eye briefly, then glanced away at the yellow sky. The heat pressed down on them, pushing them into the earth. A small dust devil whirled briefly out in the field. The load of dust it collected gave the appearance of a water spout.

"Chaw?

"Nope, gave up tobacco. Need other things more."

"This is my last plug. Found it under my pillow Christmas. Been savin' it."

"I'll have a bite of that, then."

A coyote trotted from a brush-lined ditch, out onto the field just disked. It barely glanced at the two men, not bravado, just intent on inspecting recently disturbed earth. The coyote's tail drooped low, reminding Claude of the fox tail that dowdy Mrs. Jones wore flung around her neck.

"So there you are. Where you been old dog? He usually follows right behind the tractor, catches a lot mice that way."

"Not many mice this spring. Haven't seen the owl for weeks."

"Must have moved north."

"Likely. Haven't seen a cloud in days."

"Nope, me neither. Checked the spring down in the draw yesterday. It's dried up."

"Damn! Never knew it to dry up before. I've depended on it for a cool drink ever since I was a boy."

"Yep, me too."

"It's gettin' close."

"Yep. Early and late in the day you can see two shadows."

"Noticed that the other morning."

"Some say it's bigger than the sun."

"Others say it's big enough to go around the sun and all the planets."

"How fast is it headin' our way?"

"Don't think it is. We're fallin' into it."

"Gonna be hot."

"Seems likely."

# PETITE SUITE AMICALE
Robert Wexelblatt
Volume I, Issue 4

1. *Duo Expérimental, Clopinant et Fâcheux, pour Clarinette et Bason*
Fritz's love affair with Luisa, Luisa's with Fritz, lasted most of a year. She is an actuary and a dancer; he, a chemist and poet. We all thought they were well matched. They must have believed it too. Anyone could see the physical attraction. She would lean against him and he would find excuses to touch her. Intimacies sprang from their proximity like violets in April. Their conversations appeared to be of equal interest to both. She admired his poems, particularly the ones he wrote to her. He was enchanted by the modern dance she did with the new amateur company she helped form. Their politics were just different enough. She introduced him to Thai cuisine, and he persuaded her to love Mahler's symphonies. They spent two long weekends with each others' families; his lauded Luisa, hers esteemed Fritz.

They looked certain to wed. We all expected it, and so, we presumed, did Luisa and Fritz. But they put things off, even held on to their own apartments.

One day Luisa let herself into Fritz's place—she had her own key—and found the draft of a new poem on his desk. He showed it to me later. I made a copy:

> She lifts off her blouse, shakes out
> her hair, goes on chitchatting the
> immediate while undoing
> her brassiere; elbows out, head turned.
> She is nonchalant in her nakedness.
> He scarcely watches, half-listens as

> *she steps into the bathroom and*
> *turns on the shower, hot and hard.*
> *(Always before, never after.)*
> *Curtains soak up the Brooklyn*
> *afternoon. In the street a diesel*
> *idles on and on; traffic snarls*
> *on the avenues. A clock and two*
> *fresh tampons tell the time.*

It was titled "Routine."

Naturally, Luisa was shocked, briefly. Then—and this was the greater shock—she felt relieved.

When Fritz walked in fifteen minutes later, Luisa gave him a peck on the cheek and sat him down on the couch.

"It's not…not satisfactory, is it?"

Initially stunned, Fritz said with alarm and chagrin, "You found that thing I was writing last night, didn't you."

"Didn't you want me to?"

Fritz kept his mouth shut.

"Look," said Luisa, arms crossed above him, "I feel the same way. The sex really *has* become routine. I find I'm attracted to other men, quite a *lot* other men in fact. You too?"

"Me too," mumbled Fritz. "Women, I mean."

She nodded, sat down next to him, and took his hands in hers. "It's good we found out, good we're *admitting* it. We're so much attuned it's actually no surprise we feel the same things."

"But I don't want to lose you."

"Me either." Luisa rubbed his hand as if trying to start a fire. "I know it's an impossible cliché but can't we go on being, you know, friends? The best of friends?"

"I don't know. Maybe it's not impossible." He got up and began pacing in front of her, professorial. "Others can't do it because of… let's say incongruence. One wants out, the other to cling. To be friends you need a balance of feelings. Friendship needs balance maybe even more than love does. People who break up, stop sleeping together, feel they're in a false position."

"Vertical?" she dared to joke. "No, I'm sorry. I suppose you're right."

"You and me, Lu, we're congruent."

"What do you mean, *congruent*?"

"It means being in agreement. Comes from geometry, I think." He went to the open dictionary on top of the book shelf, searched, read: *"Planes and solids are congruent when they coincide with each other after a rigid transformation."*

"A rigid transformation? Is that what we're doing now?"

"I suppose so, Lu. We reached the same conclusion at the same time, didn't we? That's got to be rare."

"Very rare."

And so, they tried.

Luisa began seeing other men. Half a dozen of them, in rapid succession. All the while she kept in touch with Fritz, phoned him, went out to dinner with him, told him as much as she would a girlfriend—more. And he was as open with her, called her as often as she did him. He worried about her and she was anxious about him. Fritz started a relationship with Marcia, a third-grade teacher he'd been fixed up with by one of us. They hit it off.

Late one night Luisa called Fritz. He was in bed with Marcia who half-woke, then turned over. He took the phone and crept into the bathroom.

Luisa was weeping. "I miss you. Oh, Fritz, everyone else just *smells* wrong."

Fritz did his best to calm her down, told her it was just a momentary regression, reminded her of why they weren't together. He knew what she meant about the smell; he was upset too, but held his ground. He was afraid that Marcia would wake up.

After that Luisa stopped phoning. Fritz went on calling her but mostly she didn't pick up. When she did she was guarded and made a point of asking after Marcia.

Fritz and Marcia began to have disagreements. It began trivially— what movie to watch, Mexican food, one of his ties—and plunged down from there. At first, he just wanted to complain to Luisa but soon found himself pining for her. It was hard to tell her so, almost too hard, but he did.

"I miss you, Lu. I *more* than miss you. We made a mistake."

"Well, one of us did, anyway."

Luisa was with Ben by then. Ben had been miserably married; now he'd been divorced for two years. He adored her. He even took ballroom dancing lessons to please her.

"Old routines?" Luisa said coldly.

Last week I went out drinking with Fritz. Over our third single malt he took a folded piece of paper from his jacket and handed it to me.

"Think I should send it to her?" he asked, ashamed.

> *The desert rushes from the oasis*
> *like ocean from a tossed rock, its bleached dunes*
> *delicate as arctic waves. Sand erases*
> *all trace of dancing, silence muffles tunes.*
>
> *Desert assaults the fragile oasis,*
> *moist thesis is threatened by a magnitude*
> *of dry antithesis. Still the heart races*
> *at the scent and thirst melts to gratitude.*
>
> *This desert is irrefutably true,*
> *yet so were the refreshing well, the dates,*
> *the vital speck of green. That, my dear, was you.*
> *The rest, I've learned, is vacancy and waste.*

At the top he had written "My Sahara."

2. *Mouvement des Parques Pour Six Instruments à Vent, Soutenant, Potinant, Amer*

Amy proposed they call themselves the Coterie of Norns and Fates because there were six of them, because she was into mythology that semester; moreover, they were all drunk and had been trashing the males in their lives as well as a number of females who weren't there. "We'll cut their threads. We'll nourish the roots of Yggdrasill," Amy exulted. Cecilia, Julie, Monica, Helen, and Megan humored her.

"Is anybody Scandinavian?" shouted Monica, looking around.

"Or Greek?" Julie giggled.

The dorm room was crowded and stuffy but they felt it as cozy and safe. The door was locked. They tumbled on the twin beds as they would have at a slumber party five years earlier, relishing collective regression even more than the two bottles of peach schnapps and the Stones' *Some Girls*.

"*Am I rough enough*," they chanted. "*Am I rich enough?*"

"Blood sisters!" cried Monica, fumbling in a drawer, extracting a sewing needle. They all punctured their index fingers and, laughing like maenads, smeared blood on each others' cheeks.


After the second divorce they decided they should be a support group, which meant meeting four times a year and talking in detail about the human beings they hated. "And then he said…Her *nose*… My mother can't understand…The guy's armpits…If only my father hadn't been…And my boss's *daughter*…Susan's awful brats…My first husband's mother-in-law…" Before they began moving all over the map they met at restaurants or bars in the city. Girls' nights out. They told each other how good they looked and foresaw great futures for each other.

The year they all turned forty, Monica suggested they gather at a resort in the Berkshires in October. The foliage. "Well," she said in her email, "we're all embarking on the autumn of our lives, so I figured."

"October, though," Helen shot back, "not November."

"Noted."

Most of them were settled. Four were mothers. Amy was almost famous. Cecilia, still single and struggling, went without cable, new boots, steak and lattes for three months to pay for the trip.

They checked out the men in the lobby, found them all wanting, played a game with the women: which were wives, which mistresses? Monica and Helen went for massages; Amy and Julie worked out. Megan generously took a hike with Cecilia; massages and elliptical machines cost extra.

On their last night Monica—who had pulled out the needle two decades before—made a crack about Julie going to church every Sunday with her sanctimonious hubby. Julie took offense and told Monica she should do something about those varicose veins. Cecilia was aghast but too poor to speak up. Helen, Megan, and even Amy were not horrified at all. In fact, Amy—their nearly famous intellectual—opined that maybe they had been too careful of each other all these years, too—and here she made air-quotes—*supportive*. They tore others to shreds but spared each other and perhaps that wasn't so wise. "Resentments fester," she said. "Look, it's the last night. Why don't we give ourselves one hour, just one hour to let it all out, I'm talking total honesty, really clearing the air, and then we'll have a drink together—peach schnapps, if you can stomach it—and then off to bed?"

"That's an awful idea," moaned Cecilia.

"No, no. It's a great one," said Monica. And Julie, still smarting from the criticism of her husband's harmless religious mania, agreed. Why shouldn't everybody suffer as they had?

Cecilia was right. There were no shots of peach schnapps, nor any more reunions. They scattered to lives which now felt colder, smaller, and irremediable.

3. *Printemps/Hiver: Pastorale Peinturant Pour Violoncelle, Flûte, et Oiseaux*

Though Paul Vareille, five years a widower, enjoyed feeding himself, he sometimes drove his big old Mercedes down to Nice or up to Grasse for a meal, especially on rainy weekdays. Though he did not frequent any establishment often enough to qualify as an habitué, he was usually greeted as one, though most discreetly. The locals respected his privacy.

As a young man of twenty Vareille did not dare to stare frankly at girls as he did now; then he had been adept at gawping without appearing to do so. However, having now attained the biblical limit of three score and ten, he felt licensed.

"I'll have the scallops and some green beans, Mademoiselle," he said to the lovely blonde waitress. "Also a glass of white burgundy, if you please."

"Certainly, M'sieur."

There were flashes, thunderclaps coming from the sea or the hills.

"God is taking pictures," he had once heard a child say. Moments later rain began to gush over the striped canopy outside; big drops bounced noisily on the tin tables. It washed the iron chairs with their Belle Époque curves—chairs like women, thought Vareille, Colette chairs. A picture of a restaurant in a summer downpour might be interesting. Grays and whites, subdued yellows over black. A mauve sheen on the cobbles. If you use it right, color can make sounds.

Vareille was shy of cameras, all publicity. He had abruptly terminated his last interview a dozen years earlier with this remark: *To let one's work speak for itself one must obviously hold one's tongue.* In Paris, he saw his dealer and certain collectors, went to a few openings; he loved walking but kept to himself. He got on well with his neighbors, tradesmen, and waiters. The farmhouse near the Côte had been left to Mathilde by her favorite uncle. She had spent her August holidays there as a girl. Vareille held on to the place and had a small studio built at the bottom of the garden, rough boards painted green, long windows, a skylight. Madame Crépellier came in three times a week.

Chloe Chatuchat, nineteen, an art student with a summer job by the shore, was used to being noticed. She wondered briefly if the old man might be a roué or a pervert, he stared so. Still, he didn't look twisted. He was lean and well dressed, and he had quite a good face with only one chin. When she stared back at him—a challenge—he did not look away, the way men with lewd thoughts do. No, he broke into a smile.

She brought him his glass of wine.

"I must apologize for my scrutiny, Mademoiselle. You're very pretty."

Unable to think of anything else to say, Chloe replied, "Thank you."

"You're a good waitress—but you're not a waitress, are you? If I may ask, what do you do the rest of the year?"

"I'm an art student, M'sieur. I just finished my first year."

"Ah," he said. "If you make as good a painter as you would a subject…" He trailed off with a gallant French shrug and an even more gracious smile.

Three days later, he returned, even though the weather was fine. He timed it so he would arrive after the luncheon rush, when people would have gone either to bed or to the beach. After she took his order he asked Chloe if she would do him the honor of sitting with him while he had his lunch. She looked toward her boss, lounging behind the empty bar with *Le Figaro*.

"Why not? Unless some one comes in."

"But of course."

She took a seat. He wondered how she would look with her hair down and concluded, better still.

"Tell me about painting. Is it painting you're studying?"

"Oh yes. Painting."

"How do you paint? I mean what do you wish to say to the world through your painting?"

"Oh, to the world!" she laughed and raised her hands. "Nothing so grand. I merely want to make good pictures, to see with them."

"To see with your paintings?"

She nodded but did not explain.

"You like school?"

She pouted winningly. "It's okay. They're giving me discipline. Color theory, layering, brush technique, oceans of art history—what schools can give."

"Do you paint outdoors or indoors?"

"Both."

"Do you also sketch? Draw?"

"I've always drawn. Since I was a little girl."

"I see, Mademoiselle…Mademoiselle…?"

"Chatuchat. Chloe."

"And did you have a hard time convincing your parents to let you study art, Mademoiselle Chatuchat?"

"Monsieur…? Monsieur…"

"Paul—"

He would have given his full name, but she interrupted him and began to speak rapidly and forcefully. "Well, Monsieur Paul, I wasn't about to let them stop me. My father's a physician. I believe he considers my ambition pathological. Mother is indifferent to anything I do so long as I marry a man with what she deems a more than sufficient income."

Vareille did not correct her misapprehension. Very well, he would be Monsieur Paul. Instead, he asked her whether she had yet met the man with a more than sufficient income.

Chloe shook her head like the adolescent she so recently was. Then she chuckled.

Vareille finished eating and leaned back, rubbing his stomach. "Well, there's plenty of time for that. I wonder, Mademoiselle Chatuchat, if you could describe one of your paintings to me."

"Are you really interested?"

"I like some paintings but I can't understand most of them. Perhaps if I too had gone to art school I would."

She told him about a picture she had done in February. It was of a goldfish. "The glass of the bowl was difficult. I included a reflection, too. If you look closely, you can see my face."

He was back the next Thursday and they chatted again, this time about Godard's films, her favorite books, and about their childhoods. Chloe found that she liked Monsieur Paul a great deal. He looked at her the way a grandfather might if he hadn't laid eyes on her for a decade. *My how you've grown—you're quite a young woman!* She felt safe with him and, what was more, like herself. Generally, with old people you had to behave like a child because that is how they see you.

He told her about his wife, Mathilde, and about the farmhouse.

"Would you like to see one of my paintings?" she asked.

"Very much. And would you like to see my farmhouse?"

"Yes, I would."

"Well then, are you free on Sunday? I could pick you up in my car. It's very big. Perhaps you could bring your painting and some drawings? And this time, I will serve lunch to you."

"I am free, and I would like to see your house. I never get out of Nice; it's either this place or the beach. And I do have some work to show you."

"Say eleven-thirty, then? We could meet here."

When he pulled up at the restaurant she was waiting. She wore a yellow sundress and was holding a drawing pad as well as two rolled canvases.

"It's a Mercedes!" she cried through the window.

"And nearly as elderly as I am," he said.

Lunch was vichyssoise, a salade niçoise, a baguette with camembert, fresh peaches. Vareille had made lemonade because the day was sultry.

Chloe ate heartily and admired the old house, also the garden.

"What's that?" she asked, pointing to the studio and biting into a peach.

"Oh, just a shed," he said.

"But it has a skylight."

He shrugged. "A little caprice of mine."

She showed him the drawings first. They were quite good and the subjects varied: a meadow, the head of a young woman, a bird, mountains and a valley.

She was delighted by the golden finches that darted down to his feeder. All afternoon, the heavy air was lightened by birdsong.

"It's lovely here."

"Yes. I'm glad you came."

"Now the paintings."

The first was a still-life: fruit, the obligatory bottle. It was creditably executed, though, the cell phone notwithstanding, academic. He saw the errors but said nothing about them. He complimented her.

"It was for school," she explained dismissively. "An exercise."

It was the second canvas that pulled Vareille up. It was a portrait; impossible not to recognize the influence.

"It's my friend Emanuelle," Chloe said.

"The style is…unusual."

She laughed, a deeper bird song. "Not a bit original, I'm afraid. I was trying to imitate another artist. Perhaps you've heard of him? Vareille?"

"I believe I've heard the name," he said dryly.

The afternoon was delicious for them both. Their conversation ranged over many topics—politics, American films, Provençal food, Italy, Hieronymus Bosch, the names of birds and flowers, Kant's ethics.

He drove her to her door. She lived in an old stucco building with unreliable balconies.

"Well, back to my garret," she said, getting out of the Mercedes, pointing to the fifth floor. "Thank you, Monsieur Paul. I had a fine afternoon."

"I as well, Chloe."

The following Tuesday it rained and he was back at the restaurant; but this time it was mobbed. Chloe had no help and dashed from table to table, throwing him a smile now and then. However, she was nearby when a portly man and his nervous wife came over to Vareille. She heard what was said.

"Please pardon us, Monsieur Vareille. You were pointed out to us at an opening last year. The Gallerie Oppenheim? We aren't collectors—not rich enough, alas—but we're both great admirers of your work and couldn't leave without thanking you for the pleasure it's given us. No, please don't get up. We'll leave you to your lunch."

She couldn't make out Vareille's reply; but she did see that he saw her, gaping, tray trembling in her hand.

This time he could not return her stare. Yet he lingered until the place cleared out and she was free. Chloe did not come to sit with him. He had to get up and beg her to do so.

Her feelings were a mélange, a bouillabaisse. She was angry, or at least felt she ought to be, but also amused, touched, perhaps a little in awe as well.

He apologized for deceiving her. "If a deception is what it was. You see, I meet so few young people, young artists. And, well, they all know who I am." He looked miserable.

She put a finger to her chin and looked stern. "I'll forgive you, Monsieur Vareille, on one sole condition"

He brightened. "Anything!"

"I will forgive you if you paint my portrait."

He had longed to do so.

"*Not* in the nude," she added.

"Certainly not! The yellow sundress?"

He painted her in his garden and could have done it in two sittings but he stretched it to four. He cherished looking at her through his painting, the songs of birds, her dappled skin.

When the picture was finished, Vareille offered it to Chloe, but she wouldn't have it. She insisted that he keep it as a souvenir, write her name and the date on the back, and hang it in the farmhouse.

4. *Pièce de Chambre à Deux Coups Pour Trombone, Harpe, et Trombone*
Hardt happened to be walking point when they took fire from three directions. There was no high ground but plenty of rocks and high grass. He was hit immediately, once in the right thigh, then again in his left arm. He spun around and fell. Rounds whizzed over him, like mosquitoes and black flies. His guys were shouting. Then he heard the two M-240s returning fire, spraying the landscape. A pair of outgoing grenades looped over him, like lazy fly balls. Then Bellino was beside him, breathing heavily.

"Told you I had your back, pal." He seemed to be whispering, and he was bleeding too; Hardt couldn't tell from where. Bellino was wiry, five inches shorter Hardt and forty pounds lighter. All the same, he managed to get Hardt's arms around his neck, told him to grab his own wrists, and crawled with him back to the rest. There was no need to call for covering fire.

Three more grenades went off, then half a dozen men ran by Hardt and Bellino; they only stopped to take aim. Then Dowd, the medic, was bandaging his limbs, telling him it was nothing, nothing, a scratch; and then there was the helicopter and he was up in the clean, empty sky, smelling cold metal. Bellino was there too, bandaged, on his haunches and gently rubbing Hardt's shoulder. "How ya doin', buddy? Ya doin' okay?"

"Thanks," Hardt said and passed out.

They were both sent back to a military hospital. Bellino was later awarded one of the more important medals.

When Hardt's mother came to see him in the hospital she said Milla had behaved well which meant she had kept tabs on her to see if there had been any other men; it meant that when Milla had promised to wait for him she spoke truly; it meant that his mother wanted him to marry Milla and make her grandchildren; it meant that he had an extra good reason for pushing himself in physical therapy, getting out of there and limping home. "Your uncle's arranging a job," his mother said, which probably meant a snug berth on the city payroll because his rich Uncle Fred played golf and pinochle with the right men. "Now, take this," she added, pressing a small box in his hand. "It may come in handy." Milla came the next day, looking beautiful and shy, tearful and glad. He was prepared. He proposed on the spot. The diamond ring his mother gave him had been his grandmother's and, since it fit perfectly, what could Milla do but cry and say yes?

Bellino was in another wing. He was released more than a month before Hardt. When he came to say goodbye, they embraced.

"Let me know where you are," said Hardt, unembarrassed by the hug.

"You bet, buddy boy."

But Bellino vanished.

Hardt was appointed Deputy County Registrar and the Registrar was close to retirement. He and Milla bought a little house with three bedrooms, not too far from his mother. Milla gave up her crap job at a dress shop. He told her over and over how Bellino had saved his life. "Out there you've got to trust men with your life but with Bellino it was different. He was like my brother. He risked his life to save me."

Hardt knew McCray was from Seattle, like Bellino. He tracked McCray down and wrote to him. McCray wrote back that Bellino hadn't settled down. On the contrary. He hung out with a motorcycle gang, got in scrapes with the law—dealing drugs, brawling—and the only reason he didn't do time was because his public defender used his military record. McCray said he'd heard that Bellino had gone upstate and was working for a lumber company and gave the name of the company and the town but said he couldn't be sure Bellino was there. He wished Hardt well, hoped he was all healed up.

Hardt wrote a letter on official stationery to the lumber company claiming he needed to reach Bellino on government business. They sent back Bellino's address. He wrote a short note: *Milla and I got married. We're fine and have a house. Please come visit. You can stay as long as you want.* He included his address, phone number, and email.

There was no reply, but two weeks later, on Tuesday at dinnertime, a Harley thundered up the driveway.

Bellino was all leather and hair; he looked like a wild man. Hardt hugged him and sat him right down to eat. He put him in the room his mother had picked out for the nursery. The first night Bellino slept in Hardt's old Boy Scout sleeping bag; the next day Hardt bought a bed for him.

"He scares me a little," said Milla softly in bed on Wednesday night. "He's so…disorderly, so *unpredictable.* You know?"

"He saved my life," said Hardt. "He's my brother."

"I know."

Bellino stayed only three days.

When Hardt came home from the office on Friday, Bellino and the Harley were gone. So was Milla, who had left a short note for him on the dining room table. *I'm sorry. Remember, he saved your life.*

# Rotting Fennel Bulb and Four Days Until

Samara Ferris
Volume I, Issue 3

I waited.
All year.
To have this much time to myself.

Two days after you left to visit your family
seven hundred miles away
I danced naked around the apartment,
I brewed my favorite rose tea,
I masturbated—loudly.
All of the things I do anyway
except this time I did them
with a feeling of ownership,
of having this whole apartment to myself,
to savor.
Every minute action,
every false-wood-panneled piece of this place
became:
regal.

After I do everything I want to—
which isn't much—
I fall into this grey void.
No dinner to make and no one to talk to.
Nothing to be cleaned and no work to be done.
No one to fill myself with.

I feel like breaking down onto the floor
into a coiled heap of warm body
drowning out the silence.
The covers on the bed are fussed
but there are no oily marks,
no loosened belts or strewn socks.
No life where your body laid
at night, next to me,
for this past year.

All my plans seem dull
and metallic.
Cooking for one feels pointless
so I melt into your leather chair
and eat raisins for all three meals.
Making dinner used to be my favorite part of the day
but really,
it was touching you.

# INTO THE WOMB OF WOMBS
Christian Crocker
Volume I, Issue 2

—not making a sound. Like a water lily trapped atop a rippling tide.

She bobbed upon The River. She recalled folklore her grandfather had longago told her. Remember *The Quieting Moon*? Remember father Sun? Child Earth? Remember the title heroine? Remember her? She was dressed for the occasion in her favorite white nightgown. Clinging wet and gossamer to the roundness of her pregnant belly. Weeds and algae floated through the water below. Drawn to gleams of dull light glowing upon The River's flowing skin. Blood wheeled in the ancient undercurrent (glug, glug), invisible within The River's impenetrable blackness. Like a spill of ink in an inkwell.

Moths trudged through muddy dusk-light above her. Landing exhaustively on tree branches.

When she was an Angry Littlegirl she hunted muddy dusk-light moths. She pinched them. Rubbed them between her fingers. Ground them to mere motes of gray silver powder. Upon which she wished. Blew from her little fingers like fairy dust.

*I wish I wish I wish from an endless wishful lish—t.*

Then watched as the flecks lingered magically in the air as phosphorous once-moths.

Granting nothing but small regrets.

A moon drifted through her routine in the sky. Like an old maid accustomed to the chores of the house in which she has worked and lived for all her life.

A constellation lay down on the bedclothes of the nightsky. Whispering. Confidingly.

Twin willows draped their limbs downwards over The River. Combing tenderly the upper current They once danced with her in ethereal winds, the willows. They once sang to her in harmonious lows and highs. Longago. When she was yet a Little Fish with gills like mermaids and rusty scales like dragons and eyes encased in black glass and featherless wings in the stead of fins like flightless dream birds.

[First Verse]
*Come up come up! Scrap the gills and scales,*
*Grow plump arms, and raise them unfurled sails,*
*Grow knotty knees, and awhile crawl on all fours,*
*Through the dirt and dust of earth's unkempt floors*
[Second Verse]
*Come up come up! Shed those featherless wings,*
*Shed those big black eyes, your ocular rings,*
*Come now, give skin a whirl,*
*And go greet your world as littlegirl*

Like that.
They had sung.
In verses like fishtails.

She remembered when she was Ugly-Age, when she would investigate her reflection, shifting her face with fingertips, remolding her features ("Your nose is much toomuch."), her grandfather, Storyteller, took her on a boat ride up The River to show her her father's new bridge. Explaining, in his grandfatherly breath, which steamed like teakettles and smelled of dusk-light mothballs, the two worlds in which she must live.

That often times she would be torn between.
Town.
Herself.
"But *you*, mydear," he declared. "*You* will always be right."
She saw The Bridge that her father built long before. That connected east Main Street to west Main Street. That the romantic Abner (One Name) had described in a poem that appeared in the *Arts* section of *The River News*,
*The metallic Brobdingnagian,*
*Sprawled over the banks of our riling incision—*

*The River that dissects dearTown in halves.*
*They rise their Giant, observe with jeering derision,*
*Nature recede through the cacophony of their own laughs.*

They rowed right under him, Brobdingnagian. They saw bats clung to his under arms, swinging sleeping upside down. Like black warm-blooded fruit. Barn swallows dove (duck) and glided just over their heads (phew). Drawing out invisible perimeters of where *they* were allowed. Before sweeping upwards, disappearing into the Giant's darkened underbelly. Like fathers will.

"Why are they attacking us?"

"Because they're afraid."

"They don't seem afraid."

"Fear is a funny thing, Little Fish."

Buildings thrived like wild reed upon a sheer ridge to the west. As the boat sailed underneath and *good* by, one of them stuck his tongue out at her. Like a teasing child two-stories tall.

"Did you know, Little Fish, they were once made of wood, the buildings? But then a fire started in the old Town House Hotel, where naughty things happened. And poof—they went up in flame."

(His eyes were ancient glossy and sky blue. Like a melting window through which a perfect day awaited.

He was born in a whole other century. Before Little Fish roamed Land. Water. Boat. Sucking up *air* air and riverwater air. When they built teasing children two-stories tall out of wood. And burnt them to the ground when they were naughty.)

The language of Hammers echoed up and up and up from upstream. Translated by a littlegirl in a little rowboat downriver.

*Thud. Thud. Thud.*
*What wary*
*Work.*
*Work all the day before the shadows*
*Lurk.*

Up in the lint-blotted blue sky, ahead of the boat, the outline of an iron half-arch carved out into the air. Clasped to granite walls one hundred feet high.

A concrete leg soaked its foot in The River's bath.

She tested the water with her fingertips.

Leftover crumbs of light glinted upon the surface. Like lures.

Warmenough.

Silhouettes of workingmen marched two by two, three by three—*hurrah, hurrah*—out onto the arch. Like ants.

*O' Creators, strong-armed and hard-willed,*
*Small gods of the world they together build.*

She imagined what would happen if the arch faulted. Snapped from the granite wall. She thought of the marching, workingmen's faces. Whiskered. Chiseled. She imagined what their last words would be, the men's, and to whom they would be told.

But couldn't bring herself to listen.

"Some words are meant for only one person to hear," her mother had said. "And you have to respect that privacy."

She deemed *this* one of *those* occasions.

*And they all went marching down and*
$$d$$
$$o$$
$$w$$
$$n$$
$$a$$
$$n$$
$$d$$
(Glug glug!)

The smells of melting metal and dull translucent kerosene came closer, drifting everywhere around the boat. Like a littlegirl's wandering thoughts.

*Thud. Thud. Thud.*
*What a wary*
*Fate.*

                    *Work all your years*
*Until your years are too*
*Late.*

Months ago, she attended a Town Meeting with her mother in the grand ballroom within The Courthouse. Across the street from the steeple bell that rang every hour.

Once for one. Twice for two. Thrice for three. Like that.

She had seen the bell on her way in *not*-ringing.

(A bell under which, many years later, she would make love for the first time. Her sighs lost behind the cry of a tolling noon.)

Her mother dragged her by an arm. Towed her close to her hip.

They got lost in oil lamp lit halls. With proud paintings of longago-men in suits and ties and white beards. "Of once-importance," her mother called them. There were plaques denoting memorable dates. Numbered doors that her mother had *no* luck opening.

Her mother finally asked a Mustached Man for directions.

This way. That way.

Backwards. Forwards.

Up the stairs. Through those doors.

Her mother plunked her down in a pew aside her handbag.

"I'm going to say hello to your father. Watch my bag."

Instead she watched her mother sway beautifully. Through standing-men conversing in a language Guardians-of-Motherly-Purses couldn't understand—not yet. Like Bird.

Her father was seated cross-legged upon a chair upon a stage at the forefront of the room. She wondered if her father would ever have a proud painting hung on an oil lamp lit wall. In some oil lamp lit hall. She wondered if her mother would too consider him "of once-importance." Her mother met her father upstage. He hunkered to his knees. Pecked her on the forehead. Said invisible words in her ear. Which traversed hilly canals and beat on faraway drums. Inspiring her mother to laugh. *Pop. Pop.* Like dissolving soapsuds.

Her grandfather had gifted her a salmon-hued shell. When she was yet a dispossessed Little Hermit. She carried it with her everywhere ever since. Stowed hidden in her armygreen satchel, her home away from home.

He taught her (among other things): When pressed to her ear the sounds of the world would fade away—hus*ssssssshed*—behind static wind. Revealing in a demonstration the shell's effect.

"You're lying."

"What? I can't hear you, Little Fish."

"I *said*: 'You're lying!'"

When she returned to the pew, her mother tapped her shoulder. Her look said *put that away. We're about to get started.* And so, a magical shell was demanded back to the bottom of an armygreen satchel.

Her father talked from a podium.

"I've given it much thought, and—," her father said. "I propose we entitle the new bridge, The Long Bridge."

*Hmms* made their way around the crowd. Like donation plates.

"Of course, naturally," her father continued. "We would have to *re*title The Bridge, The Short Bridge, as to save ourselves any confusion."

Puffy huffs drew over the ballroom sky. Like exasperated cloud cover.

> *Thud. Thud. Thud.*
> *What a cruel, cruel*
> *Sound.*
> *Destined forever to be the boss's*
> *Hound.*

"Is that The Long Bridge?"

"Not yet. But will be very soon."

She undressed and bellyflopped from the boat. Rinsing the dryness of toomuch *air* air from her face.

When she was Old Enough To Know Better, she thought she

would drown without a balance of *air* air and riverwater air. Which, according to her grandfather, was what fish swallowed upup and spit outout. Like toomuch fat.

One day her mother had found her upon her back upon the grass behind the house. Breathing heavily and slow. Not making a sound. Like a dying bullfrog at the base of a washbasin. Her mother panicked. Swept her into her arms. Like too many things to handle. And rushed her into the kitchen.

"I need to go to The River, Moo-Moo," she gasped. "Take me to The River."

"What will that do? Why can't you breath?"

"Because I'm drowning."

Her mother set her down. On two littlegirl legs.

"You're pretending?"

"No."

A palm slapped her. Like a fishfin.

A purple palm print leeched through the surface of her cheek. Like it had been hidden underneath her skin. Always. Lingering in burial, waiting for *this* moment to come and pass. Always.

She swallowed *air* air upup. All the *air* air in the house. All the *air* air in the world. Her lilypad-green eyes shined wet. Like two mossy stones thun*ked* upon the bed of a pond.

She ran from the house. Leapt from the back verandah. Like a once-dying bullfrog resurrected. She spit *air* air outout. And gobbled it back upup. Decorations from a once-living room adorned the backyard. Lawn ornaments commemorating her birth. The Era of Her Parents Getting Accustomed to Their New Lives With Child. Her Post-Pre-History. When nurseries were fashioned from old rooms transformed. When houses had to be rearranged to make room for her. When there was, for instance, *no* room for books upon a shelf, a green velour sofa and crates of toomuch stuff.

She dove off the dock with the tied-off rowboat, and into The River. A flotsam of froth above traced her movements below.

Willow voices met and swam with her. Beneath her beneath the water.

[First Verse]

*Sometimes we do such awful things, don't we?*
*Sometimes we aren't nice, and we can't explain why,*
*Can we? Sometimes we want to hurt whom we love most,*
*And hate to hurt them, but we still do,*
*Don't we? Don't we?*

Underwater the ancient undercurrent whispered by her. *All worlds*, it spoke, *begin* (glug glug) *with a single breath* (glug glug).

But that's what the ancient undercurrent always said.

Then vanished (glug glugging downstream).

Her head surfaced buoyantly. Polished. Shining-wet. Like sad eyes. Coughing riverwater air outout. Inhaling *air* air inin. Her grandfather helped her into the boat. Wrapped her snugly in a white towel. Like a future dusk-light moth cocooned.

Moo-Moo, her mother, was called Moo-Moo because seared upon her belly was the word *Bishop*. Longago pressed into her skin with a branding iron. When she and her mother would lie together in bed, whispering confidingly, she would rest her head on Moo-Moo's chest. Draw up Moo-Moo's blouse. Outline Moo-Moo's brand with a finger.

"What does it mean?"

"*Bishop?*"

"No, to be branded?"

Bubba, her father, was called Bubba because he misconstrued her first word.

One morning he tucked her in her bassinet. Played with her chubby-whubby toes. Observed her drift in and out of baby sleep. When he began to toe from her nursery with the mustard colored walls, with the baby bird photographs on the ceiling, with her birth announcement cut from *The River News* framed upon one wall (*Baby Born Baby Girl*), she cooed it.

He raced downstairs. Skipping steps. Nearly almost-falling. He found his wife on the back verandah. Rocking in her chair. Not making a sound.

"I'm Bubba!" he declared. "Me—Bubba!"

The week prior, when her father was at his office in Town, and her grandfather ventured to the house to recite to her a fable, her mother eavesdropped from outside the nursery. Seated on the floorboards in the hallway. Not making a sound. Reliving her nighttimes when she was a littlegirl herself.

"*Into the Womb of Wombs* goes," her father began. As once he had begun longago. "*Into the Womb of Wombs* goes."

The story varied from the one her mother remembered. The narrative he told then was about a salmon born magically in a river. A strange fish, with gills like mermaids and scales like dragons and eyes encased in black glass and featherless wings in the stead of fins like flightless dream birds. And how the fish transformed into a littlegirl. And how the littlegirl would grow up and have Little Fish to call her own. And in that way life progressed.

"Did you enjoy it, Little Fish?"

*Yes,* her mother thought. *I loved it.*

Then a soft voice cooed from within a mustard-colored painted nursery one little remarkable word, one little remarkable name.

"Bubba."

Her mother would never have the heart to tell her husband the truth.

And would vow her father to silence.


Her parents married in 'nineteen. A year before her father would be commissioned to design and build the first bridge. And two before a babygirl would be born a salmon in The River.

Her mother's favorite aunt, to the chagrin of *her* little brother, sat in a back pew swabbing her ear with cotton cloth.

"At the very moment my daughter is reciting her vows," he said. "All you can think to do is scrub your ears."

A Justice of the Peace officiated, because neither believed in god—not yet. (He *would* only later. In the moments before his death. And she *would* only in the moments *after* his death. To hate Him.)

Years later, her mother would recount when *that* tear performed a pirouette upon her nearly-husband's cheek.

"Was he sad?"

"I don't think so."

"Then why would he cry?"

"*Because* you are."

*Yes, yes.*

*I do* .

*I do.*

She wiped the tear from his cheek. Lining her lips with it.

Rings bound golden around their ring fingers.

*Husband. Wife.* Like that.

Cheerful clapping awoke the silence in the mothy, dusk-light air within the wedding-hall.

They walked up the red-carpeted aisle. Ring-hand in ring-hand.

He smiled teethly and shook guests' hands.

She licked her lips. Tasting the soluble Something Borrowed dissolve away on her tongue.

Her mother would show her photographs from the ceremony and the small reception that followed.

They interested her, the photos. *When did Moo-Moo look like that? Whenever was Bubba known to wear a suit and tie?* The old album was titled (or was it—branded?): *Our Big Day.* They would sit around the dining table for hours, her and her mother. By the end, the photographs would collect fine littlegirl fingerprint smudges and would need to be dry wiped clean with cotton cloth.

She would keep two of them. Always. They would travel with her in life. Always.

1) Just-hands cutting with a knife a first slice in a one tier, white-frosted wedding cake.

"Whose hands are those?"

"They're mine and your father's. Our bodies are out of frame."

"Why?"

"Because a camera only wants to see so much. Can only capture what is most important."

She resolved that day to live her life like a camera.

2) A car. *So Long* had been painted in white across the trunk. Her mother perched in the passenger seat. Waving *So Long* through the rear window. Mere fragments of her father caught here and there: A hand on the steering wheel. Some hair on his head. His own much toomuch nose. Through the front windshield the road was welcoming yet terrifying.

> *Was the car moving?*
> *Why wasn't all of Bubba important enough?*
> *Moo-Moo, is that Bishop Road?*

On her own wedding day (her first), she would attempt to recapture *that* photograph precisely. Yearning to recover a metaphor she had seen when studying the original with her mother She would direct the photographer. She would direct her then husband. She would style her hair as her mother's hair had been styled. She would smile as her mother had smiled. She would paint *So Long* across the trunk of the car. (The car's model, she hoped, would be the only discernable contrast between the original and her refashioned attempt.)

In the end, however, she could conclude only one thing with certainty: The car must have been moving.

Her grandfather drew in the oars, and the boat hesitated. Like *not-breathing*. Then began to drift downstream. Away from the *thud thud* protests of hammers. Away from workingmen marching from tumbling not-yet bridges.

Storyteller was called Storyteller for Obvious Reasons.
Bubba had been stolen and employed. And he told stories.
The End.

[First Verse]

*Come up come up! Scrap the gills and scales,*
*Grow plump arms, and raise them unfurled sails,*
*Grow knotty knees, and awhile crawl on all fours,*
*Through the dirt and dust of earth's unkempt floors*

[Second Verse]

*Come up come up! Shed those featherless wings,*
*Shed those big black eyes, your ocular rings,*
*It's time now for skin to employ,*
*And for you to greet your world as littleboy.*

Like that.
They sung.
In verses like fishtails.

# CREAM RISES:
## Lana Hechtman Ayers in the Service of Poetry
Michael Dylan Welch
Volume I, Issue 3

Lana Hechtman Ayers, who lives in a waterfront home south of Kingston, Washington, across the Puget Sound from Seattle, is a regional poet garnering increasing national attention. If you saw her at a Seattle poetry reading, you would find her to be warm and friendly, her brown eyes sparkling as she greets one poet friend after another with an embrace and a ready smile. While many poets will trip over themselves to get to the stage as quickly and often as possible, Lana is frequently happy to facilitate, to showcase others' work. She does this not only in readings, but also in her service as a manuscript doctor, poetry editor for *Crab Creek Review*, and editor/ publisher for the Concrete Wolf poetry chapbook series. She holds BA degrees in mathematics and psychology, an MA in counseling psychology, and an MFA in poetry. It has also been my pleasure to curate the SoulFood Poetry Night in Redmond, Washington with her since July of 2006. She is an accomplished poet, with a long string of publication credits, including *Bitter Oleander, Feminist Studies Quarterly, Poetica, Potomac Review,* and *Slant.* She has also published several books of her own poetry. Despite her seeming reserve, in print her words are transcendent, often startling, sometimes fierce. Lana Hechtman Ayers is a poet of increasing braveness who, except in this rare interview, lets her poetry do her talking.

**What motivates you as a poet?**
　　The answer to this question is the same as if you asked me

why are you living—to make sense of life, to make meaning, to connect, to make life better for others. Writing poetry is the way I discover and express my humanity. I want to write about what I've experienced in various ways in the hope that doing so creates common feeling, understanding, new perspectives, or perhaps a sense of shared experience.

**Some people might think that parts of your education are "unpoetic." Please talk about your educational background and how its diversity contributes to making you the poet you are today. You say on your website that you'd like to go back to college some day to study astrophysics!**

My undergraduate degree in theoretical mathematics is probably as close as one comes to poetry without using words. Theoretical math is a very beautiful language whose aim is to describe, comprehend, and express the world more fully. What is more poetic than that? Trying to make sense of the world is an extraordinarily poetic endeavor whether done via words or equations.

I also possess a second Bachelor's in psychology and a Masters in counseling therapy. Again, another attempt to make sense of life— my own and to help others make sense of theirs. This is the main aspect of my poetry.

And then there's the MFA. I went for an MFA precisely because I had no formal training in poetry. I had been reading poetry since childhood, willy-nilly, whatever captivated my attention. I wanted to know about all the poets and poetic disciplines that came before, what they did and why and how. I felt I owed it to myself as a writer to get this formal training so that I could better understand how to craft my own poems and better communicate whatever it was in me that wanted to be said in poems.

I've always been a searching for meaning. I've always wanted to know more about the world—how it works and our place in it. I think all these degrees are consistent with that poetic drive and hopefully have made me a richer individual to come to the work.

**Please share a few favorite lines of poetry, of any era, or several eras, and say why they matter to you.**

Oh my gosh, where to begin? So many poets, so many favorites. I guess I will give you my early favorites. From the poem "on a Gift of Watermelon Pickle Received from a Friend Called Felicity" by John Tobias in an anthology we read in grade school by the same name, the first two lines:

> *During that summer*
> *When unicorns were still possible;*

Those words hit me hard at the tender age of seven because I was already nostalgic for a childhood I never had, a childhood where anything seemed possible, a childhood of joy and imagination. That wasn't possible in my household.

Also, in that same anthology, which I imagine would never be given to third-graders today, was "Résumé" by Dorothy Parker:

> *Razors pain you,*
> *Rivers are damp,*
> *Acids stain you,*
> *And drugs cause cramp.*
> *Guns aren't lawful,*
> *Nooses give,*
> *Gas smells awful.*
> *You might as well live.*

At the age of seven, I had wished to die many times because of my circumstances at home. Ironically, this poem gave me the courage to keep living. Here was a woman who knew pain, and like me thought about ending her life. She not only lived on but became a successful writer. This poem told me that there were others in the world suffering like I was and that if I could just hold on, I could be okay some day too.

Here is the blisteringly brilliant last stanza from Emily Dickinson, poem #640:

*So We must meet apart—*
*You there—I—here—*
*With just the Door ajar*
*That Oceans are—and Prayer—*
*And that White Sustenance—*
*Despair—*

What speaks to me in these lines is the idea that connections can occur across time and distance that are deep and true and necessary. These connections can open us up, sustain us or even drown us. The voices of poets across time and distance were my "door ajar." Even despair itself can be a lifeboat. As long as you are feeling, you are alive. When I first read this poem as a thirteen-year-old, I understood the words from inside my gut.

And finally, these opening lines from T.S. Eliot's "Four Quartets," which I read when I was fourteen:

*Time present and time past*
*Are both perhaps present in time future,*
*And time future contained in time past.*
*If all time is eternally present*
*All time is unredeemable.*

Eliot's poem felt very profound to me at the time but I couldn't say I had much comprehension of it. And though I didn't know what to make of it entirely, parts of it felt wrong and angered me. I had read poems that moved me and poems that didn't. But this poem both moved me and angered me at the same time, which was very confusing. It felt very negative about humankind and life on earth. I didn't want to believe my life was unredeemable or that the bad that happened to me early on contained future bad. Wasn't the fact that I was writing about my pain some sort of redemption, I wondered? So naturally, after this encounter with Eliot, I turned to Plath. Ah, preaching to the choir.

**How does the Seattle poetry scene differ from other parts of the country? What would you make better here? And what are the biggest strengths of the community here that you would wish for other places?**

I've only really lived in two places as a practicing poet—southern New Hampshire and the Seattle area. Naturally, population plays a role, but in the Seattle area, if you wish to, you can attend a poetry reading every day of the week. Some days, there are so many overlapping events you are forced to miss out on some. Many of these reading are also open mics, which are an occasion to connect with other poets in the area. I have found the poets at readings to be friendly and inclusive. After I had just moved to Seattle, you were one of the many kind folks who offered information and resources to me after I heard you read at the It's About Time Writer's series in 2004. There's also a terrific writer's center called Hugo House (www.hugohouse.org) that offers writers an alternative or complement to academic courses of study. I met many of my dearest poetry friends by taking classes there. I tell people you can't toss a pen in Seattle without hitting a poet and it really does feel true. The community is vast and diverse. The only thing I would wish for the poetry community here was that there was more interweaving of the different groups—youth, spoken word, academic poets, poets of differing ethnicities and races. There is some, but I think more exposure to one another would feed and inspire everyone.

Southern New Hampshire has fewer opportunities to attend readings or open mics, and the events are spread out over a much broader area. When I lived in Nashua, I was a founding member of Poets Unbound, a poetry critique circle that met weekly at the public library. I also took classes taught by eminent poets like Ottone Riccio, Patricia Fargnoli, and Kate Gleason and connected with writers in those classes. The New Hampshire Writers Project (www.nhwritersproject.org) is also a wonderful organization that provides opportunities for writers to connect. I have taken note that many new venues for readings have arisen than when I lived there, and that's very encouraging. Poetry is alive and thriving in southern New Hampshire.

**When did you first become aware that words and writing and poetry mattered to you? Who are some of your poetic influences, past and present? You dipped into this topic when describing favorite lines of poetry previously, but tell me more.**

I grew up in a home with a functional mentally ill mother who was emotionally, physically, and verbally abusive. I was a scared, shy child who didn't understand what was happening to me and I felt I couldn't tell anyone because it was somehow my fault. I turned to books for relief and escape. I discovered a volume of poetry by Rudyard Kipling in a basement when I was five or six and read all the poems aloud. I didn't understand what I was reading but I felt when I was saying the words aloud they had a kind of magic, like a spell or prayer. I knew, then, words were sacred.

In addition to the influences mentioned earlier (Tobias, Parker, Dickinson, Eliot, Plath), in my teens and beyond, I glommed onto Sharon Olds, Adrienne Rich, Edna St. Vincent Millay, Elizabeth Bishop, Wesley McNair, Patricia Fargnoli, ín Espada, Lucille Clifton, and Stephen Dunn. It was more recently I discovered Pablo Neruda and Lorine Niedecker, as different as any two poets can be. Neruda is lush and Niedecker succinct and I relate to both forms of expression very deeply.

**You've published your books with relatively small independent publishers. How important is it to you to work with indie publishers, and what are the pros and cons? In general, what could independent small publishers do to get their books more widely known and appreciated?**

I haven't chosen to work with small publishers. They chose me and I am very grateful. Small presses can't afford publicity because there is so little profit (and often loss) in poetry. Amazon.com helps somewhat as does the web and social networks. As a small press publisher myself, I use all these avenues and am looking into making books available for e-readers. I have worked with some lovely presses and have felt like a family member there. I imagine it doesn't feel quite the same at a large press but you do have better odds of your words reaching more readers. I like to be optimistic though. I think no matter who publishes your book, your words will make it into the hands of the readers who need them.

**Is a poem ever finished or just abandoned?**

I've abandoned hundreds and hundreds of poems because no amount of editing would ever make them feel right to me. The poems just didn't seem to be saying something that mattered in an artful-enough way. I always hope that eventually I will find a way to say what needs to be said in a new poem. Then there are the poems that I have to put away for a long time because the emotion is too raw to really get the craft straightened out right away. And always some poems of mine appear in print that I want to tweak. Sometimes when I give readings I actually do cheat and change them a little. Oftentimes, I find myself hating my published poems when I look at them years later, wishing I could have done better. But I think this is natural. Creative people are always growing, so the you that reads your poem ten years hence is a lot different from the you that wrote it. Just as we are never finished growing until we die, I suppose our poems aren't done evolving either.

**You have been an editor for *Crab Creek Review* since 2007. What is your process with the journal, and how would you describe what pleases or surprises you and your coeditors. How much of a Northwest flavor does the journal have, would you say?**

For me, reading the submissions is such a gift. I never take lightly the hope and care that goes into every envelope and I deeply appreciate that those writers are entrusting me with their words. Ronda Broatch and I read every poetry submission that comes in. We then bring poems to the editorial staff meetings with editors-in-chief Kelli Russell Agodon and Annette Spaulding Convy to decide collectively which poems go into each issue. And each of us gets to pick poems we love even if some of the other editors don't agree.

Being the first literary journal to publish a poet is one of the most exciting things there is about being an editor. It strikes me as being akin to an astronomer discovering a new galaxy. I am sure every poet who has sent work out recalls his or her first yes. Mine was from

George Loon, and I will always be grateful to George for believing in those two poems that had been submitted a dozen times before they found their home with *Lake Effect*.

*Crab Creek Review* has been a well-known journal in Seattle, having been created more than 25 years ago by poet Linda Clifton. But it has been a national journal for two decades and gaining acclaim and appeal more and more with every issue. So although we receive a large number of submissions from regional poets, we receive more than half our submissions from all over the country and overseas as well.

Our main goal is to publish a piece of writing that, as readers, we want to read again and again, a piece of writing that stays with us.

**As a poetry book doctor, with the services you offer through Night Rain Poetry, could you talk about what you look for in a book of poetry, and what you try to give it to make it a proper book rather than just a collection of poems? What makes the difference? And what are the varieties of ways that can make a book work?**

Making a book a book is a very intuitive process for me. Because I am not the author of the poems, I don't have any history, chronology, or emotional attachments to the work. I can see each poem for its words on the page and am able to see how one poem speaks to another. I make arrangements that feel like a journey or a series of journeys. And it's crucial that early poems invite the reader into the experience.

Oftentimes, poets put poems in their manuscripts solely because those poems have been published in journals. Prior publication should never be the sole criteria for a poem to make it into a collection. Another common assembly problem is simply putting poems in a manuscript in the order the writer wrote them. Sometimes this will be fine, but most often not.

There are many ways to make a book manuscript flow. Tone, imagery, emotion are just a few that work well. But the most important thing is that every poem in a manuscript must carry its weight. There can be no filler whatsoever. If a book contest says they want manuscripts of 60 to 90 pages, I advise clients to send 60. Less is always more when those 60 poems are sailing the reader on a great voyage.

**Please talk about some of your other activities in poetry, such as your Late Blooms poetry cards, or the annual Poetry Postcard month. What rewards do these and other poetry projects provide to you? What other kinds of writing do you explore?**

Poetry has literally given me my life and makes my life better. I often say kindness is my religion and poetry is my spiritual practice. It feels then like a necessity to me to give something back. For me it's a kind of tithing to run a reading series, or to facilitate a poetry postcard fest or publish chapbooks.

When putting poetry manuscripts together, less is more. When putting poetry into the world, more is more. I know this seems contradictory. I just want to help in every way I can to get more poetry by more poets into the world where those poems can do so much good work.

The August poetry postcard fest was originated by organic poetry guy Paul Nelson (poetrypostcards.blogspot.com). The goal of the project is to get people all over the country and the world to send a postcard poem a day to 30 different people on a list, hopefully in such a way that each poem you write is in response to the postcard you received in the mail that day. I just love the idea of a postcard poem winging its way through the mails to arrive as a gift in some stranger's mailbox. Immediately a connection is made in just a few lines and images.

I've always been a lover of novels and short stories. Since completing my two poetry collections about Red Riding Hood and her associates, which are stories told in verse, I feel a tremendous pull toward writing fiction. I've been working on some short stories and thrown-away attempts at two different novels but I am determined to keep exploring.

**What words of advice would you have for an aspiring poet? What about for poets who have published to some degree?**

Keep writing and keep reading. That's really good advice for everybody no matter how much experience or success one has at publishing. Keep trying to improve your craft by studying writers you love, taking classes, finding peers who can give constructive feedback.

I always quote my grandmother when giving advice about getting published: "cream rises." What she meant by that was that good work gets noticed. I believe this to be true.

**What's next for you and your writing?**

After my brother died last May at the age of 53, every time I sat down to write, the poem was about him. After hundreds of brother poems, I got a little worried that I would never be able to let go of him or my grief. So I stopped writing poems for a while to focus on fiction, in which, miraculously, no one I loved ever died. But I have now realized forcing myself to stop writing poetry was absolutely the worst thing to do. My heart is even heavier than it was and I feel like my entire life is on hold. So for National Poetry Writing Month this April, I have committed to several poetry friends to write at least one poem a day about my brother. I have a feeling I'll write more than one some days. And I may continue to write about him for months and years to come. Ultimately, I know writing our truths, even scorchingly painful truths, is healing and life affirming. How did I ever manage to forget? So, I am not giving up on my poetry for fiction. I will forge ahead with both and go wherever the words take me.

# REMEMBER SHE WHEN
### Charity Hestead
Volume 2, Issue 3

| | | | | |
|---|---|---|---|---|
| Remember | when | Seattle's | sky | broke |
| the | mountains | thin | dusting | lost |
| way | collapsed | buildings | gathered | lovers |
| she | and | shattered | pedestrians | stood |
| looked | all | the | while | together. |

Remember the way she looked
When mountains collapsed and all
Seattle's thin buildings shattered? The
Sky, dusting, gathered pedestrians while
Broke, lost lovers stood together.

Remember when Seattle's sky broke?
The mountains' thin dusting lost
Way. Collapsed buildings gathered lovers.
She and shattered pedestrians stood,
Looked all the while together.

# DOCUMENTARY
Caleb Krause
Volume I, Issue I

The crow is an assembly line.

First it waits

Then it scavenges

Then it eats

And talks

And hides

And eats

And flies away to live on dying trees.

It talks about average things

Like how much it rained yesterday

And how it likes this cloudy weather

And how it hates the small berries

Because they are harder to see.

When it makes love it's just for fun

Because it doesn't care about

Its species going extinct or

Cooking breakfast for two.

When it laughs
It's at the expense of other crows
That's the kind of humor crows like
That's why they always eat in groups.

Years ago
When I use to smoke
I would go outside on cold Decembers
Near the dumpster
And watch them from a distance.
That's how I know.

# Wake Up Dreaming
Stephanie Mabey
Volume I, Issue 2

*"So, this is what you do?"*

The question caught me off guard. I had just played five of my most finely crafted, shiniest pop songs for a major music publisher who, until that moment, had been quietly listening with his head down.

My stomach sank. "Yeah. This is what I do."

The meeting was over in 25 minutes. I ducked into a parking garage and cried for at least that long. It wasn't just the letdown of an unexpectedly disappointing meeting, but because I knew that getting so close to what I wanted shouldn't have felt so empty. I should have walked out of there saying, "Yeah. This is what I do." Completely believing it. Those five songs were the ones I thought a publisher would want to hear, written for people who I thought would want to sing them and it would have been satisfying…if it was what I did.

I went home and threw myself into the music I was passionate about. I gave myself permission to figure out exactly what it is that I bring to the table as a songwriter and artist. Expressing universal themes through left-of-center perspectives had become my outlet for my creativity in the midst of trying to write a *hit*. So I gave the cast of misfit characters floating around in my head the attention they deserved. The bearded lady who found love. Zombies. Villains. A self-destructive robot. I didn't write these ideas as novelty songs. Each concept was a musical gauntlet I threw down to challenge and express myself. I stopped seeing my songs as darts crafted to hit an invisible mark set by someone else and really began focusing on what I had to say.

Six months ago I was sitting at my keyboard and started working on a dreamlike piano riff that I couldn't get out of my head. It snowballed into a song about a comic book artist who works at Office Max. When I was done writing it, I realized that the thing I wanted all of my music to say was right there in the title. *Wake Up Dreaming*. I had found my musical mission statement. I took a recording of it with me to a music conference and played it for various industry reps. I sat across the table from music supervisors and publishers as I did before, but this time I wasn't worried about their response. I knew that this song was the start of a new chapter in my music. This was the song that would help me find the kind of people I wanted to work with and the kind of people I wanted in my world. This song was my bat signal.

The response was overwhelming. People were cuing in to what made the music different and fresh and they were excited about it. I went home with an arsenal of contacts that the song resonated with. My whole perspective had shifted and the side effects were far-reaching. I started getting more freelance songwriting work than I'd ever received before. I had a few tracks included on an album that was distributed to over 50,000 people. I was able to raise the money I needed to start a new album. I found myself being fueled by the response of new fans who were discovering my songs online and at shows. The more I genuinely believed in what I was doing, the more people could get behind my music. This sounds like such a no-brainer, but it took me months of actively working to trust myself to reach that point.

A couple of weeks ago, my little sister played me the first song she wrote on her ukulele. I was floored by how great it was, but she answered my enthusiasm with a hasty "I'm not really a songwriter, but thanks." I begged her to let me record it for my blog and YouTube channel. I wanted to share her creation with my fan base. Then it hit me. I want to use my blog to do the same thing I want to do with my music. Encourage people to wake up dreaming. I keep noticing the fascinating people around me that are doing more than just existing. They're creating and adding to the world around them. There is a kid who lives in my apartment complex that's building a crazy go-kart contraption from pieces of scrap metal in his garage. Every time someone drives by, he looks up and smiles like "Go ahead. Ask me." I plan to. Now I'm actually excited to get online and promote not only my music, but a concept I'm truly passionate about. I want to remind the people around me that we can do what we really love in spite of any odds we have stacked against us.

We don't have to choose between making a living with our art and being true to ourselves. Sure, it can be incredibly easy to get lost in the midst of our struggle to pay our bills or to feel validated. I've been there. I didn't realize how far I had gone down that path until I was sitting on the pavement between two cars, wondering why I had spent so much time creating music for the sake of meeting someone else's quota. But I've also experienced the forward motion that comes from digging deeper into my craft and truly finding my voice. I have seen the pieces falling into place faster than ever as I've let myself write the music that I always wanted to create.

I am so glad my heart was broken in that publisher's office ten months ago. It allowed me to step back and discover who I am as a songwriter and artist. I'm taking more risks and creating songs that I fully believe in. I'm still very much at the beginning of this new chapter, but I can't wait to see where it leads.

My name is Stephanie Mabey. I am a 26-year-old singer/songwriter from Denver. This is what I do.

# WAKE UP DREAMING

He sells office supplies in his nametag and tie
They complete his secret identity
Unknowing citizens shop for ballpoint pens
To them he's just the guy who rings them up

> He can't shake the feeling
> That this whole world's asleep
> He's full of vision no one else can see
> But soon he'll make it real
> 'cause he knows how to keep believing
> Wake up dreaming

On fifteen-minute breaks he fills his sketchbook page
With characters sworn to protect the earth
And they save humankind from evil masterminds
They're his only hope in a sea of envelopes

> He can't shake the feeling
> That this whole world's asleep
> He's full of vision no one else can see
> But soon he'll make it real
> 'cause he knows how to keep believing
> Wake up dreaming

He keeps sketching fire escapes and back doors
Knows there's got to be more to his life

> He can't shake the feeling
> That this whole world's asleep
> He's full of vision no one else can see
> But soon he'll make it real
> 'cause he knows how to keep believing
> Wake up dreaming

# Such a Lovely Girl
Zach Hively
Volume 2, Issue 2

"Gramma, are you gonna put peroxide on it?"

"Shush you, Melanie." Grandma Chrissy always fusses like a mother cat around my daughter. "I done what I needed to do to get you cleaned out. You got yourself just a scrape that isn't any deeper'n the water in my rain barrel out back. See, look at what you got on that rag. That ain't nothin' to get yourself so worked up about."

I look over at the cloth in Chrissy's hand, at the blood and puss and dirt, and I flinch. Looks like damage enough to me. Thank goodness Chrissy is here to be the nurse. Hopefully the gashes won't scar.

"But Gramma." Melanie's little eyebrows scrunch and the tears that had begun to congregate on her bottom lids quickly fan out across her lenses without so much as a drop spoiling the flush of her cheeks. She already has big brown doe-eyes without that extra sheen. Looking at them melts me every time. "Your barrel has lots of water in it. Didn't you even hear the rain last night? It came down for a whole hour!"

"Well." Grandma Chrissy reaches for a tube of antibiotic ointment to spread over the torn and tender pink skin on Melanie's knee. "With all your water balloons, I never figured you kids would have left a drop—"

The back door of the double-wide slams open and Buck runs through. He skids through the kitchen and brandishes his cell phone like he's a rookie cop on a TV show, trying to prove himself. He's too young to have that phone anyway. His elbow bashes Melanie's shoulder, but Chrissy catches my girl's thigh and keeps her from tumbling out of the chair. Melanie shouts at him, "Watch where you're going, Buck!"

"Slow down, Buck! You're going to hurt someone again."

The kid stops to gape at me. "You can't tell me what to do, Uncle Flynn. You're not my dad."

Grandma Chrissy takes her free arm and pulls the squirming Buck to her chest like a football. "Buck, I seen your grandpa move like that before, and it ain't never meant that he was up to somethin' good. Now tell me just what has got your britches chasing you down like that and I might think about forgivin' you for running through my kitchen."

"Gramma, Gramma, Gramma." Buck swallows. He sticks his cell phone in her face, a modern-day Paul Revere forcing his technological distress call on the elderly. I can see that the cause of his alarm glows dimly on the little screen. His grandma nudges the arm aside and raises her eyebrows to ask *what, what, what?* Buck struggles to break free and reach the front door. "Brad said, Brad said, Brad said...they hit a, hit a, a deer!"

I twist back around to the window over the kitchen sink. Behind me, Chrissy says, "Who did? A car?" The chair creaks as she shifts. "Buck, you better mean a car, 'cause if one of you boys done *anything* to harass those deer—"

"Not the boys, Chrissy," I mutter. I can just see the highway out the window. "A truck. It stopped up there." I've never seen deer as frequently, or as close, as I have ever since I started driving down here with Caitlin in our first year together. Her parents always have stories about the deer, talk about them like they are neighbors. And they are beautiful, and graceful, and all of those things that I always imagine in wildlife. "I can't see what it hit."

"Not one of our deer." Melanie's firmness makes me look at her over my shoulder. She breaks from Grandma Chrissy's knurled and tender hands with a spastic force and her feet reach the floor before I think of how to respond.

Buck takes advantage of his grandma's distraction and he sprints through the rest of the kitchen and out the front door. He's probably more anxious now to get away from Grandma than to see the deer. Melanie shoots to the door right after him on her scraped-up legs, and

I step around the kitchen island to follow her. I hear Chrissy's chair when she separates herself from it.

Melanie stands just outside the front door, where she stopped running. She's trying to take everything in and probably doesn't even realize that she is swaying, as if moved by a gentle breeze that exists only for her. Where the green metal gate is fastened open at the top of the driveway, the rest of the family has gathered just inside the fence line. Buck darts in to join his siblings; their mother looks like a vulture disregarding her flock of carrion-picking chicks. I can't imagine any of them are hesitant to approach the carnage on the highway. So why do they stay just where my little Lucas can flit around them like a lost quail? Even Caitlin stands there looking across the road instead of making sure our son is not picked on yet again by his cousins.

Melanie's Uncle Stan and Grandpa Timothy suddenly stand up on the far side of the highway, their upper bodies now visible over the thin line of asphalt. The deer must be right there. To the left, the pickup on the shoulder has at least one set of headlights bashed out that I can see. The orange turn signal dangles from the truck by its wires, like I always imagined a poked-out eyeball would look. A man I don't know, presumably the driver, fusses with something in the bed.

Stan and Timothy walk back to the pickup truck together after studying the deer. I nestle the ball of my hand between Melanie's shoulders. "Do you want to stay down here with Grandma?"

"No, Dad. I want to go up there with everybody else."

"Flynn," Chrissy says from the doorway behind us. She's trying to imply some meaning that I don't grasp. Probably she wants to shelter little Melanie from the scene that waits up on the highway as badly as I do. Though I could be wrong, and I don't want to risk right now being one of our moments.

"Okay." I take my hand away from Melanie's back and she moves toward the driveway with small yet certain steps. Grandma Chrissy crunches through the gravel until she joins me. We walk behind Melanie toward the rest of the family.

"Thank you for doctoring her in there."

"Shoot. Don't even mention it. I'd do anything for that girl." She pulls her shoulders up around her neck, as if shielding herself from some phantom chill. "It's just torn skin. We all get scraped, and we all get healed up again. It's part of being a kid."

"Did she tell you who pushed her?"

"She didn't get pushed by no one. She tripped and she fell down. It happens."

We reach the top of the driveway, but Melanie continues going past everyone else. She stops just on the other side of the fence line. Chrissy goes to say something to her other grandchildren, who look to be joking about guts spilling from their bellies. Caitlin pads over to me, wraps her arms around my waist, and tucks her forehead under my chin. She whispers:

"Oh, Flynn. It's so sad. You never get used to this sort of thing."

"Is he dead?"

"She. And yes. Thank gosh, she at least died right away."

"Well, that's something, at least."

The sound of air tumbling over an oncoming car reaches us before the sound of its engine does, and before we can even see it. The sedan rockets past us, the sound ripping through the silence we had created. Its passing seems to snap existence back into place. The regular rhythms of the desert country, all as shocked as I am from the death of an innocent animal, recover their senses. And I seem to regain mine. As the car fades away to our right I can hear the murmur of voices from behind the pickup truck across the road. I notice the trill of some bird or insect that for a moment reminds me of the Volkswagen Beetle I had as a teenager. I never had to worry about wildlife in the road, but with the way I drove, I probably should have wrecked at least once. But hell, drivers were different then, and I thought I was invincible. Bloody gauze would not have touched me. Not now. More is at stake. A creature has died, my girl is naturally curious, and like always I wish I could mute the insensitive and indifferent babble from my niece and nephews. Whatever Chrissy had to say to them, they won't listen.

"Dad and Stan moved her off the road already," Caitlin murmurs. She, too, seems to have been jolted back to life, though I think she's still more affected than nature itself at the disturbance. "She's right over there, between those two Apache sagebrushes."

"Can you do that? I mean, don't you have to call the police or something first?"

"We did that already. A trooper's on his way out."

"And wasn't there a mess? Did Lucas see it?"

"No, she didn't tear open. Of course Lucas saw her. He was playing in the yard with his cousins and they beat us up here. But he didn't see anything bad. Just a deer."

"One of them pushed Melanie over."

"I'm sure it was an accident."

"Were you watching them? Because clearly your sister-in-law was—"

"Flynn. Not again. Not now."

Melanie turns back toward us. Her feet still point to the highway. "Mom? Dad? Can I go see?"

"Baby," Caitlin answers first. "Are you sure you want to do that?"

I cut in. "Melanie, I don't think you really need to see what's over there."

"Dad," Melanie says, as if what she's about to say is the most obvious observation. "I'm nine years old. I think I can handle it."

"Okay, sweetie," my wife says to her. "But you go over there to Grandpa first."

Melanie nods. She walks up to where the gravel driveway fades into the slant of the asphalt shoulder. I don't hear any more cars coming. She looks both ways, just like we taught her, and then walks carefully across the two lanes.

"At least Lucas is too busy to want to follow his big sis." I squeeze Caitlin. "I'm going to go over there, too."

"Honey, have you ever seen a dead deer before?"

"What, you think the city boy has never seen a dead animal?"

"Well. Have you?"

I let go. "Not up close, no."

"Are you sure you're up to it, sweetie?"

"I'll be fine. Promise." I kiss the top of her head and follow my daughter.

I get one foot across the white line before I remember to look both ways.

Melanie has already placed herself square between her Grandpa Timmy and her Uncle Stan, and looks like she thinks she's one of the boys. She's got her hands on her hips and a cocksure tilt in her stance. I half wonder if she's about to spit on the shoulder of the road.

The driver turns to me when I walk up, and whatever conversation was happening dies down quick. I slide my hands in my back pockets. "So, how's the truck?" I try to sound casual, but it doesn't work.

"Alright." He reaches over the truck bed and slams shut one of those lockers or trunks for holding tools and stuff. "I've seen worse."

"We're just glad you're alright," Melanie says, with a bit of the twang her grandparents always wear on their vowels.

"Thanks, kid. Me too."

"Yeah. That could have been a lot worse for you."

The stranger looks at me like I'm an idiot. Which I suppose I kind of am. I decide to recover myself. "I mean, at least you were in a big pickup truck. Just imagine if you were in a little car. A Prius, or an old Bug."

The stranger stares at me, and then spits on the ground. Timothy navigates back in with a sentence that makes no sense to me, but must be a continuation of the earlier conversation I had interrupted. The three other men form an exclusive triangle of dialogue of which I am clearly not a part. And somehow, Melanie just fits right—

Melanie is not here.

Look around everyone—no Melanie. Did she run off? I look back to the driveway—no Melanie there. The sound of a car—is it coming toward us? I open my mouth to yell for her, but I see Caitlin looking at something down the road. I follow her eyes and there, a hundred feet or so away, is my little girl, standing erect and alone next to the carcass.

Of course. She wanted to see the deer.

My heart still pounds, and I want to sprint over to her and whisk her away. I start to jog. But I see the way Melanie looks next to the animal, the bearing she has, and I slow to a timid walk.

I wish I could know what was going through my little Melanie's head. She is always so inquisitive and always so precocious and always so smart. And always so polite. Yet she feels in ways I have never seen in a human being before. I don't want her to see this deer, because I have a sense of how the image will slice her tender insides. I don't want my girl to be scarred.

But I can't keep her from knowing. She has already seen the deer, now. I can only tend to her wounds if this moment cuts her like I think it will.

What is that look on her face, though? She's feeling. I can see her eyebrows furrowing, even from here. She isn't studying the animal like a scientist. But she's not weeping over it, either. Not like her mother might have done.

Now I too can see the deer. Her lips are parted. Not limp in death as I expected, but firm, ready to pull bark from a tree or call to its herd. Or is it called a flock? I don't even know if these creatures make noises, let alone what to call their families.

I'm close enough to touch Melanie, to rub her shoulder and pull her into my side and make her feel alright. But I'm not sure it's her that needs comforted. I sense that this is her moment.

The doe's eye, the one that we can see, has a tear of blood frozen in time where it ran down her cheek.

The asphalt tore the fur from her skin like old burns, scarred over with time. It ripped the thin flesh from her front knees and exposed the bone, which I think at first is just more skin. I have never seen bone inside a creature before. Only on shelves in the back science room at school, or in museum display cases, or maybe in a butcher's shop. My own arm quivers at the idea of uncovered, fleshless bone. And I can only look away from the incredibly dainty knees, exposed here to the sun and the stuttering wind, to set my eyes upon the doe's belly, swollen already to bursting like a mockery of new life.

Drips of blood hang glistening from her teats like fresh milk. Like she is waiting for the fawns of death to drink from her.

Melanie steps in full circumference around the doe, from head to legs to the still-playful flip of a tail. The furrow on her forehead is if anything deeper than before, but I can understand her thoughts as well as I can the doe's.

A car comes straight at us. Adrenaline flushes through me. I reach across the deer for Melanie. I can't get to her. Then my flight instincts chill out when I realize the vehicle has slowed down. Rubber crackles on grit as the state trooper's SUV pulls close to us. The officer exits his vehicle. Melanie once more holds herself like a proud nine-year-old girl. "Hello, sir," she says to the trooper.

"Hi there." He takes the most cursory glance at the doe, and says, "Damn things are spendin' too much time by the roadside. At least the drought keeps 'em from breedin' too much. You folks feed the deer?"

"No, sir. The neighbors did that once and it brought a mountain lion to their porch."

I swear, this girl remembers every word her grandma tells her. Every story is gospel.

"That's what happens. We'd all be better off without the deer. It's a shame they get in the way."

"Yes, it is, sir."

I keep my own mouth shut. The last thing I want to do is say something stupid in the presence of this doe. The trooper strolls over to the three men around the pickup truck.

Melanie steps over to me and takes my hand. "You ready to go back with Mom and Gramma?"

"Sure thing." I squeeze her hand and we look both ways before crossing back over the highway.

"Did you see her eyelashes?"

"No, I didn't."

"How could you miss them? I wish you'd seen them."

I don't know what quality her voice carries—longing, perhaps, or wistfulness, or an innocent yearning without ache and disappointment—but I notice it. Whatever her tone, it makes me wish that I had been able to see them, too.

"She had the most beautiful eyelashes I've ever seen. She was such a lovely girl, Dad."

# MY BEST FRIEND POETRY IS AN AWFUL COOK

Michael Patrick McSweeney
Volume I, Issue 2

My best friend Poetry knows how to turn the dials,
to invigorate the electric oven,
but when I tried
to teach him the art of boiled water
he burned his hands and cowered
against the counter, clutching
his raw, twitching digits.

To be honest, Poetry
is the sort of person who prefers watching others
cook ribs on a sooty grill,
because the process takes five hours
and he can drink the whole time.

I remember one night, when trying to cook
shrimp scampi for two: Poetry
told me he would decrust the crustaceans
while I used the bathroom.
When I returned I found the poor prawns
mashed into an incomprehensible pile.
Poetry cackled, clapped his hands,
and spread shellfish around like the cold.

At the sight of me he fled, leaving the door open
so it would catch the wind outside, slam shut.

I spent twenty minutes
alone at the dinner table,
balancing a fork on my index finger
and using a steak knife to carve my initials,
but it was useless:

I went to bed hungry that night.

# DEAR MR. BRADBURY
John J. Walsh IV
Volume I, Issue 2

"Live forever!" It is the commandment that defines my life, informs my soul. In this slowly decaying case of flesh, my mind and heart struggle to reach for faraway stars and a path that by all conventional thinking is inherently unobtainable. Yet I know there is a way, for *he* has told me, shown me, guided me.

This man who dares to smash the ticking clock of mortality is none other than legendary writer Ray Bradbury, who has loomed large over my life since I was but a boy of eleven years. What follows is the story of how simple words upon a page brought forth a hero, and how that hero became a personal mentor.

It begins in the sixth grade, a time when boys are restless, bored, and in desperate need of summer. *Jurassic Park* and its revolutionary dinosaurs had taken my imagination by storm just a few months prior. My personality and body were in a state of flux as I began to take those first wobbling steps into adolescence while still dragging forward the muddy footprints of childhood. I stood upon the crux of all the future while managing to be completely and beautifully unaware of its tremendous weight.

My teacher that linchpin year was Mrs. Mary Wilson, a wonderful woman to whom I owe much, even beyond that which transpires amongst these typed lines. The largest portion of this debt lies in the single choice of a simple action on a typical day. I can still see her taking the small paperback book from the back shelves of the classroom, walking to her podium, and sitting down upon the high seat. Her fingers leafed the pages, searching for their mark. She began to read aloud. "The courthouse clock chimed seven times. The echoes of the chimes faded." But not the repercussions of the events she set in motion that day.

The story was "The Whole Town's Sleeping" from Bradbury's collection-turned-novel *Dandelion Wine*. I was mesmerized. And when Mrs. Wilson read the final, terrifying line, I was hopelessly addicted. I asked to borrow the book so that I might devour its entirety at home. I raced through those pages and demanded more. The local library became my buffet for all works Bradbury. I read anything and everything upon which I could lay hand.

The seventh grade and Ms. Lucy Callero presented me with yet another worn book plucked from back shelves. This time it was a collection of stage plays from various writers, containing the one-act drama "The Meadow." Ms. Callero encouraged my blooming passions with an enthusiasm my fellow students probably would have thought uncharacteristic of her stoic nature, but she cared deeply for her pupils and fanned the flames of sparking young minds whenever she could.

This carried me into the eighth grade and the classroom of Mrs. Rosemary Erlinger. It was she who gave me my very first piece of authorial advice, which continues to serve me well: "Just start writing." She is also responsible for the first time I met Ray Bradbury. I had missed the morning announcements once again as a result of tardiness, a common occurrence that was largely due to my night owl habit of reading long after midnight. Thankfully, Mrs. Erlinger knew to repeat a certain special item from the day's list: Ray Bradbury would be speaking and signing books at the local library.

I shouted a yelp of joy that only a child's lungs could put forth into the world. This was a possibility that fell beyond the realm of my youthful understanding. Authors were magical beings that existed beyond my lifetime. Jules Verne was long dead and buried at earth's center, was he not? Herman Melville's words had to escape his watery grave to make their way to my shore. H.G. Wells was lost to the past, his novels a last will and testament tossed forward through time. So, thusly, Bradbury surely wrote his stories on Mars or beyond and flung them back to Earth in slick, silver rockets, words to be read by eager young boys but written by a man whose body and essence existed elsewhere, not here, definitely never to cross paths with such a mortal being as myself. Yet here was an announcement, a grand proclamation: the arrival of a god, come to Earth for a day, to reach out and touch my hand, to bless me with his speech and tell me tales of the universe that lies beyond that ethereal border which I could never hope to reach or comprehend.

I shivered with excitement the whole day. I declared the great news to my mother when she came to pick me up from school. And when the impossible, faraway future finally came to be present, it was she who drove and accompanied me to the library that night. The date was October 4, 1995, and despite it being her own birthday, it was Mom who gave me that greatest gift.

I was incredibly nervous, sitting cross-legged on the carpeted floor with so many others, surrounded by the towering stacks of books that defined much of my youth. What was once a mere building had been transformed into a grand temple that was now blessed by the presence of one of its greatest gods. My eyes widened as Bradbury took the podium, his white hair and thick glasses standing impossibly tall over me. He smiled. He spoke. My world shook.

He told stories, just as Mrs. Wilson had that one fateful day. He became my teacher, or a priest at the pulpit, preaching a love and passion for living the likes of which I had never before seen. My mind reeled at his words; it was so much to take in, to absorb, to understand. At thirteen years of age, I was standing at the edge of a cliff I could not fathom. Bradbury was instructing me to jump, to dive, to fly, but I was not yet ready. I was mostly stunned into a state of perpetual awe, during which only a few stuttered words could escape my lips.

It was my mother who asked the question that night, not me. She urged me to do so, but I was far too shy. So she raised her hand, and he called upon her. "Mr. Bradbury, is there any way that someone could write to you?" He responded by saying that we should contact the library, and they would pass along correspondence. Mom nudged me in excitement, encouraging me to do just that. But what could I possibly say? Words failed me.

Despite my shyness, I left the event with a full heart and a personalized, signed copy of *Fahrenheit 451*. I felt as if I had touched the sky for but a brief moment and was slowly floating back down to earth in a cloud of profound intoxication. It was an occasion I considered "once in a lifetime," never to be repeated, equaled, or outdone. I returned to my ordinary life, one filled with textbooks, schoolyard play, and fantastic adventures undertaken by night stand lamp light. Only my mother's and my memories, and a prominently displayed book upon the dresser, proved that I had spent an evening in the shadow of my great and mighty literary hero. I had come home to my family and he had slipped back through the sky in his shiny rocket, to that weird and unknowable place where authors roam and write their grand tomes.

If my disheveled record keeping is to be trusted, it was the spring of 2001 when Bradbury returned to our little library. I found that still my hands trembled when I handed him my books to sign, and that my tongue failed to bring forth my deepest thoughts. I felt as if struck by a whirlwind, lost and dumbfounded in a moment that I desperately wished would never end, only to find that it was already over. Thankfully, I found strength enough to ask one small, lasting favor. With the encouragement of my mother once more at my back, I stood before the table that had been set up in the small, front wing of the library and nervously asked, "Mr. Bradbury, could I have my picture taken with you?" That photograph still holds a celebrated place in my home today, and I can remember the moment with tear-wrenching clarity, as he placed his hand upon my cheek and drew my head next to his. The flashbulb illuminated the room, and my brain could not escape a singular, powerful thought: *Within this mind, so warmly pressed against my own, lie the wondrous stories of forever.*

I was fortunate enough to again see Bradbury at a public speaking event or two over the subsequent months, but it was the following summer, in 2002, when my grandmother initiated the next phase of my life by handing me a small newspaper clipping advertising three one-act plays under the billing *Bradbury: Past, Present & Future*. Having enjoyed the television-adapted stories of *The Ray Bradbury Theater*, I was enthralled at the prospect of seeing his work translated for the stage.

While I had attended and enjoyed my high school's small theatrical productions, I had yet to be baptized with the level of passion I now hold for the medium. That first evening at the Court Theatre, seeing those stories leap from the page and take limb, stirred something deep within my soul, transfixed me completely, never to let go.

I returned to that same playhouse for another set of three one-act plays, this time to find a surprise waiting for me: there in the lush courtyard was the playwright and master himself, sitting quietly in his wheelchair. I was terrified in the best way possible, for here there were no tables or podiums or stages to mark the border between author and reader. Yet, even with such an opportunity, I found myself mute.

I continued to attend each run of new plays, usually alerted to their premieres by my ever-watchful grandmother, who would lovingly scour the newspapers for announcements.

The beginning of 2004 brought Bradbury's Irish comedies to Theatre West, and I dutifully followed. I arrived early and sat on the lobby bench as I waited for the house doors to open. Turning the tickets over in my hands, my mind wandered. It was the sound of the main building entrance door opening that snapped my attention back to reality. And there, now sitting right next to me, once again quietly in his wheelchair, was the author.

We sat there in silence, each contemplating the other, for what felt like a sizable segment of eternity. I think his eyes dared me to speak, drew the words from my throat as though a caught fish. The ice broken, we talked briefly, though I nervously. I can today recall absolutely nothing specific of what we said, so loudly was my heart pounding in my chest. I felt incredibly blessed by the serendipitous moment, but slowly regret began to seep into me as I contemplated the sad possibility of never being able to truthfully transcribe my heart's contents into words of sound or scrawl.

The next two years would bring several public speaking engagements at which I would get to see Bradbury, but never in that interim did the chance to so freely interact manifest itself. My bittersweet graduation from college, a depressing cubicle job, and the slow crumbling of a failed relationship would suck the life from my spirit, creating a dark period in this chronicle which we shall simply call "intermission."

The curtain rises in late October 2006, at a local bookstore. *Farewell Summer*, the follow-up to *Dandelion Wine*, had just been released, and Ray came to speak and sign copies of his latest work. While I had brought the freshly-autographed novel from home, I did purchase a small paperback copy of *Zen in the Art of Writing*, which I did not have signed that day. The friends who joined me for the event thought it odd, but for some inexplicable reason I insisted on saving the book for later. Like a plot element left aside to hibernate, it lay in wait, ever patient.

Flash-forward to April 28, 2007. It was a day of irrepressible excitement as I took my seat in the third row of Royce Hall on the UCLA campus for the Festival of Books' Ray Bradbury panel. I had attended this same event every prior year that I was able, but somehow I knew that this year's would be special. I left the lecture in tears of joy. Something was coming alive within me that I could not explain, but my heart felt ready to burst at the seams. I have an audio recording of his speech that day, and I listen to it whenever I need to be reminded of what is most important in life.

The warm summer months introduced a new venue—the Fremont Centre Theatre—and a new set of plays, one of which was based upon the same story Ray told the night that Mom and I first met him. This small and unassuming playhouse would come to occupy a special place in my life and be the backdrop against which the future would unfold.

Soon after, as a surprise, two close friends gave me the wonderful birthday gift of taking me to the gala premiere of the Irish comedies' return to Theatre West. Ray was in attendance, as part of the event was a celebration of his own date of birth. Whereas before my stuttering tongue had betrayed me, I now began to find my form. I was finally able to tell him about that life-altering day when Mrs. Wilson had read from *Dandelion Wine*. He very excitedly told me that his play adaptation of the book was going to be performed in about a month, and that he would see me there.

At a celebration of his eighty-seventh birthday, Ray Bradbury was the one who gave me a gift. It was an intangible box to be opened later, to be contemplated, the fantastic mystery savored. That gift was unwrapped a few weeks later, upon my return to the Fremont Centre Theatre.

*Dandelion Wine* had me in tears throughout much of the play's length. The words that had so completely captured my imagination thirteen years prior were poured into the world upon that small stage. After the performance, there was a small gathering during which I had the opportunity to meet several of the actors, a company of incredibly talented individuals who would come to provide great and lasting inspiration. When the crowd died down, I was invited to sit next to the head of the one remaining table, presided over by none other than the playwright himself.

We began to talk, and I found every word that I had ever before lost. I left no thought unsaid. I professed my love, my eternal gratitude, everything you have read to this point. I told him that he was my Mr. Electrico, the man who surged lightning into a twelve-year-old Ray and gave him life and commanded him to *live forever*.

He took my hand and kissed it. As I embraced him, he kissed my cheek. I was a bastard son reunited with his literary father. To mark such an occasion, we made plans to meet again where we first did all those years ago, at my local library. Ray would call them and come give another lecture.

December 1, 2007, was a cold evening, my breath bellowing out as misty smoke in the frigid winter air. Tucked under my arm was *Zen in the Art of Writing*. I had been reading it the week-long, and the final beautiful lines fell before my eyes as I waited outside the library doors. Ray signed it that night, after another soul-stirring speech. It was a busy event, without chance to converse.

A few weeks later, on the closing night of his plays, I once more carried that book with me. Ray inscribed it with what has become the cornerstone of my life's overarching philosophy: *Love what you do! Do what you love!* That night, with those words, with that book, Ray handed me the touchstone to which I constantly return. Whenever I falter and lose step in life, this is where I go. It serves as a consistent reminder to follow my instinct and trust my creative judgement, regardless of contrary opinion. If I am doing what I love, then I am on the right path.

When 2008 began shortly thereafter, I started my true journey of discovering myself as a writer. I had written poetry and essays before, but these were all done in a largely scholastic capacity and seemed merely warm-up exercises for releasing what brewed deep in my subconscious. Following Mrs. Erlinger's earlier advice—a sentiment echoed strongly in Ray's own—I just started writing. No thought maps or concept webs or plot outlines. What emerged was a short piece that evolved into a one-act play. It was of terribly amateur quality, but it began to loosen the cork that bottled what lay hidden within myself, that untapped well of ideas.

That August, I wrote Ray a birthday letter, which I presented to him lovingly tied with ribbon to a plastic Stegosaurus. In it, I thanked him for showing me the way to finding my legs as a writer. Two days later, he called me and left a voicemail, which I play back whenever I need to be reminded of just how incredible life really is. Few things can zap me full of more energy than hearing Ray Bradbury's voice declare, "I love you very much."

In response, I sent Ray a fax. As his biographer Sam Weller once noted, "There is a room in the Bradbury home dedicated to the device." It is largely how the outside world communicates with him, and now my love-filled words were being transmitted across the telco system and into "the fax room." Ray called me back while I was in the middle of the grocery store, a surreal experience to say the least. He invited me to come to the next set of plays, said that he wanted to see me there. I would never look at the toothpaste aisle of that Ralphs the same way again.

September presented me with the inspiring impetus for my book *Of Sirens and Sand*, and brought artist, friend, and collaborator Martin Abel into my life, a subject to which I dedicated the article "Sail Together, Swim Alone" in *Line Zero*'s previous, inaugural issue. It was during this time that I truly began to look at myself in the mirror and see the reflection of a writer. The robes were still loose, but the title was starting to fit better and better each day.

The next time I saw Ray, the conversation was different. No longer were words being exchanged between an author and his reader, but between two writers, two lovers of the way a pen can glide across the page and leave worlds in its wake. We compared the joys of collaborating with artists whose works endlessly filled us with inspiration. He told me stories that I had never before heard him tell in all the years I had been attending his lectures. From this point forward, our encounters would become increasingly familiar. I religiously attended, at minimum, every premiere and closing night for each run of his plays. It never lost its luster when Ray would sit next to me, pat me on the back, and say, "It's great to see you!"

Summer 2009 brought a particularly special treat, when "The Meadow" came to life upon the stage as part of another set of three one-act plays. How I wish that Ms. Callero could have been there, to see what had become of that short play in that small book with which she had so thoughtfully presented me all those years ago. Due to a knee injury that I had recently sustained, I had to sit in the back row of the theatre, so it was not until after the play that I was able to speak with Ray, but what a conversation it was. I pulled my wheelchair up next to his, and we began talking. Other than sharing with him my introduction to "The Meadow," we said nothing of his works or even writing in general. Instead, it felt like a conversation between old friends.

Later in the summer, after Ray called to invite me once more to join him at his plays, I waited in the lobby that had become a second home. He rounded the corner, beamed a smile, and exclaimed, "You made it!" He asked me what I was writing. My answer of "prose poetry," a style learned from a lifetime of reading Ray's work, brought forth a joyous laugh from his lungs. He crossed his hand over me and proclaimed, "My spirit is with you!" We talked much more that evening, but it is this blessing which shines brightest in my memory.

I would spend the remainder of the year and the beginning of the next immersed in *Of Sirens and Sand*, working hard to live up to my mentor's proclamation. Within those months came one final Ray Bradbury stage production, a musical. "2116" stole my heart, and Ray told me that he thought it was his best work for the theatre. Tears still wet upon my cheeks, I was inclined to agree.

In the summer of 2010, Ray's theatre company sadly came to a quiet close after forty-seven years. Despite packed houses, there simply was not the funding necessary to continue. It was the end of an era which had come to define my life and writing. Ray had also hurt his leg, impairing his ability to travel. The last I briefly spoke with him was during the release of Sam Weller's *Listen to the Echoes: The Ray Bradbury Interviews*. It was a crowded event and there was not much place to talk, but it was wonderful to be in the presence of his glowing energy.

I have a picture that was candidly snapped as Ray was leaving the bookstore, when he held out his hand to take mine, looked into my eyes, and smiled. It was the same hand that had reached out a decade prior, to place my head against his for our first picture together. I cannot help now but think that it was his way of drawing my life into his own, to cast me a part in this grand and wondrous production, written and performed with a passionate love for the very act of living.

Not seeing Ray in these recent months has been hard on me. I cannot deny how deeply I miss the frequency with which I grew accustomed to spending time with him. I never took any of our encounters for granted, but now I find the memories of those blessings doubly precious. It grows heavy on me to be forced to acknowledge that there is a finite limit to the drawing of breath, that with every gushing flood comes eventually the slow and inevitable ebb. Yet I fight it.

I remember the words of Mr. Electrico, the commandment passed on to me by Ray: "Live forever!" Searching for its meaning, I return to contact the library, his answer to my mother's question years ago, and there I find him. He is waiting quietly on the shelf, with Verne and Melville and Wells, writing to me from beyond Mars, from that magical nether-place where writers practice their sacred craft. Here Ray Bradbury lives, now and forever.

Each day, I sit down at my writing desk and take small steps toward joining him in that strange place. Perhaps it will land me upon those same library shelves, my work wonderfully misfiled next to his, and there I will find such everlasting life. More likely, it will be immortality of a quieter kind, the sort of which is gently passed between the lips of generations, tumbled down family trees, resting namelessly in the laps of laughing, summer-soaked children. Whichever it is to be, neither outcome greater nor lesser than the other, it comes to me as a gift, one that Ray gave so selflessly.

As I contemplate such futures, I realize that no words, written or spoken, could ever sum up fully the debt to which I owe this man. There is no level of thanks or praise high enough to grant him the honor he deserves. All I have is my small part in the legacy he has painted upon the earth, one of his countless literary children, unleashed into the universe with a mission of love, passion, and wonder. The life I lead, the philosophies I carry forward, these are the contents of that letter I could not fathom writing as a wide-eyed thirteen-year-old boy. But were it to be composed as such, those thoughts rendered, written, and postmarked, I imagine the lines would be simple and brief.

Dear Mr. Bradbury: Thank you for the secret of living forever. It was love all along. It was always love.

Clive walked out of his house on Liberty Lane with his cup of coffee and brown pinstriped robe cinched around his waist, just like every morning. He grabbed the newspaper off the stoop and tucked it under his arm while strolling down the row of blue houses with off-white trim. Each home was identical, except for the Customized™ window placements. Clive grinned as he compared his impressive bay window to the others on the block. He inserted his credit card into the mailbox to download his e-mails and, if the rare occasion should strike, withdraw Letters©.

Everything about that Saturday seemed routine, until Clive noticed a small piece of Paper™ sticking out of a sewer grate. Clive wasn't really the impulsive type, and normally he wouldn't feel compelled to pick up a scrap of litter from the sewer, but something about that Paper™ made him curious. It was yellowed, with strange black lettering that remained flat on the surface. There was no Digi-Track© music playing as his eyes scanned the page; it was a very low-tech piece of Paper™, yet it intrigued him. The lettering was in some strange language, and Clive didn't know the first thing about translations or how to research such a topic at the Store®. However, when he flipped the Paper™ over, the image on the reverse-side spoke volumes. The picture was black and white—like one of the old still photographs Clive had seen in history class as a boy. It depicted a rolling landscape, with foliage twisting outward at irregular intervals, evidently unconcerned with size and placement standards. There were stout bushes, elongated trees with strange pointed leaves, grasses that weren't cut, and even bare patches of open dirt occasionally blotting the scene. It was all so random.

Clive glanced down the parallel rows of houses, making sure nobody was watching him. He dashed back into his house, instinct told him that this find was special and worth guarding. He pulled down the shades on all his windows. Dust sifted around the room. Clive hadn't closed his shades in years; he liked to keep them open so that his bay window was backlit and easily ogled from the street. Clive dropped into a nearby chair—speckled with a Customized™ floral arrangement—keeping his eyes locked on the picture. Even with its grayscale coloring, Clive could tell the scene was alive. He wanted to go there. He loved the utter chaos of the picture.

Although he never told anybody, Clive had always loved watching things that were not Normal®. He marveled at the way his stubble was haphazard and patchy every morning, or the way his food tray always looked disorderly after he finished a meal; no matter how carefully he ate, the crumbs and flakes left a unique-shaped mess each time. He was fascinated by those few idiosyncratic parts of his day that never seemed Normal®.

Clive ran his fingers up and down the picture, tracing the oblong outline of each tree. He leaned over and pulled back the window shade with his palm. He gazed out into his yard at the three trees allowed by the Liberty Lane Homeowners Association, each planted equidistant from the curb to his house and trimmed to prescribed dimensions. Until that moment, he had never wanted more than three trees. On Liberty Lane, like elsewhere, having a good yard was important. Those who could afford to live on Liberty Lane took pride in keeping their lawns manicured, making sure trees were trimmed, and hosting weekend barbecues. It got to the point where the Liberty Lane Homeowners Association drafted a schedule for barbecues, thereby making sure each resident got his or her share of the calendar.

Clive slid his hand away from the Customized™ window and let the curtain shroud him in secrecy once more. He continued to stare at the picture the rest of the evening, entirely forgetting there was a barbecue at Owen's house that night. As his lights automatically shut off, Clive continued to stare in the darkness, letting his pupils adjust as his eyes caressed the image. Long after the gentle, automated spray of insecticide from his Yard Management System© killed the chirping crickets—a sound which usually signaled bedtime—Clive put the picture into a frame that formerly housed a Dyna-Photo© of his grandmother. He changed into his pajamas, brushed his Poly-White Teeth™, and went to bed.

On Sunday, Clive went to the Store®. He surveyed the trees for sale, lined up in a neat row along the back wall of the home and garden department. Not satisfied with the selection, Clive asked a clerk if the Store® had any more trees.

"Yes, we have extra inventory in the warehouse," the clerk responded.

"I know that," Clive said. "What I mean is: do you have more varieties of trees?"

The clerk stared back with a puzzled look. "What?"

"Do you have any different kinds of trees?"

"I'm still not following you."

"I'm looking for trees that have different colored leaves, different sized trunks, different heights," Clive said, getting irritated with the clerk.

"No, these are all we have. These are Normal® trees. The best money can buy," the clerk said, motioning to the row of trees.

"Fine," Clive said with disappointment. "I'll take two of those trees."

Clive handed the clerk his credit card. The clerk swiped it, grimaced at the computer screen, then handed the credit card back to Clive. "Our files say that you already have three trees, and they are still perfectly healthy. We can't sell you any more. It's against neighborhood policy."

Clive expected he'd be denied access to the trees, but he thought it was at least worth a try. He trudged back to his house at a sluggish pace. He walked through his yard, not with the usual sense of pride but with disgust. Clive meandered inside his house, pulled down the shades, and studied the picture a second time. He was once again mystified how every angle, line, and varied shade of gray was utterly unique. There was nothing Normal® about the image.

Clive went to bed at the usual time that night. It was Saturday, so instead of insecticide, the spray signaling the day's end was an extra dose of herbicide.

The next morning, Clive woke up, shaved, ate breakfast, and went to work. As he sat in his cubicle—staring at his reflection on the slick, white desk, populated only by a ledger, Dyna-Calendar©, and pen holder—he could see the black and white picture's every detail staring back at him in that glossy, blank slate. He decided that if he couldn't have more trees, he could at least make his three more interesting and less Normal®. That evening, when he went home, Clive tossed his pruning shears into the hungry metallic jaws of his Deluxe Compactor™. As the days rolled on, his trees became more and more disproportionate. Some of the branches arched out, others grew toward the sun at an accelerated pace, and dead branches wilted, unpruned and unattended.

Two weeks later, Clive answered his front door to find Megan, his nearest neighbor, standing on the stoop. "Good evening," Clive said with a smile.

Megan didn't return the greeting. "You have to trim those trees."

"Why?" Clive asked.

"They're an eyesore," Megan exclaimed. "The Liberty Lane Homeowners Association has clear rules about tree grooming."

"I know," Clive said, frowning, "but they're stupid rules. Why can't I have those trees look however I want them to?"

"Because you just can't. Your trees reflect badly on the entire neighborhood."

"I'm not shearing them."

"You have to," Megan insisted. "If you won't, then I'll take this to the block president."

"Fine, you go do that."

It only took two days for Megan to get Owen, the block president, to pay Clive a visit. The conversation went similarly to the last one. One day after that, Megan stood at Clive's door again, Owen on her left side and a police officer on her right. The officer's hands were cupped behind his back, trying to appear nonchalant, but

Clive noticed the little strap on the top of the policeman's gun holster was unsnapped—ready for a quick draw if things got tense.

"Sir, you have to trim those trees. It's the law," the officer told Clive. "If you don't, you'll be deported."

"But I was born and raised here. I'm a citizen," Clive said.

"That makes no difference," the officer said, "you're being insubordinate, and we can't have that. A true citizen wouldn't want the neighborhood to turn into a chaotic trash heap. We have rules for a reason."

Clive didn't respond. He crossed his arms and closed his eyes, barely able to believe what he was hearing. "I threw out my shears," Clive said.

"Well, find a replacement. These trees must be trimmed before sundown, or I'll be forced to take you in," the officer explained.

"Owen, can I borrow your shears?" Clive asked through gritted teeth.

"Hell no, you've been acting really weird lately. I don't want you borrowing my stuff," Owen replied.

"You can have mine," Megan said with a grin. Clive hadn't wanted to use Megan's, but it looked like he had little choice. She went to her garage and retrieved the sinister clippers. Clive grabbed the monstrous gardening shears from Megan's clammy hands. Her grin exploded into a smile. "You can keep them," she said. "I've got an extra pair."

The next morning Clive woke up, but for the first time since puberty, he didn't shave. He let his stubble remain in its patchy beauty. He didn't want to impress anybody. He hated his yard and his newly clipped trees. He wanted to be transplanted into the black and white photograph, far away from Liberty Lane. That Sunday, Clive stayed up late reading and rereading the neighborhood charter. He went to bed to the hissing sound of liquid fertilizer spraying across his yard.

On Monday, Clive inspected his facial hair with pride. Some of the patches had filled in. He didn't go to work. He opened his shades and let the sunlight pour over him as he sat in plain view and studied the picture. He read the neighborhood charter again, then he returned his gaze to the old grayscale picture, then to the crisply-printed charter once more. He went back and forth like that all day. When his neighbors returned from work, they gave Clive strange glances through his Customized™ bay window. The sun set and the moon shot into the sky. On Mondays, insecticide was the spray of choice as Clive drifted to sleep.

By Tuesday afternoon, Clive found redemption in the charter's legalese. He went into his basement and disconnected his Yard Management System©. Clive went to bed that night with a smile, as silence replaced the usual hissing chemical sprays emanating from the yard. The next two nights were soundless too. Then, on Friday, when the insecticide was usually reapplied, Clive heard some crickets return to his yard. It always amazed Clive how fast the crickets converged on his yard, even after so many were killed every few days. Normally, the Yard Management System© disposed of each new batch of crickets right on schedule, but this time, the insects remained all night. The chorus of crickets rose louder and louder, until reaching an apex like Clive had never heard before. By the time dawn struck and the crickets' tune lulled, Clive hadn't slept a single minute. It was such a beautiful song, and Clive longed for the music to return as he lay in his bed with bloodshot eyeballs peeled.

Within a few weeks, Clive noticed dandelions sprouting in the tall grass that he hadn't mowed since disconnecting his Yard Management System©. He'd received messages from some of the neighbors, asking if he was alright, seeing if he needed help with his yard work, or wondering why they hadn't seen him at the office. Clive didn't return any of the calls, and nobody came to his house to chat.

It wasn't until about a month later that Megan led a group of neighbors onto Clive's property. Their boorish approach trampled dozens of dandelions. Clive opened his door to greet them, hearing the group's ruckus long before they rang his doorbell. Clive's unkempt beard caused a few of the neighbors to gasp. "Clive, what's wrong with you?" Megan asked.

"Nothing," Clive responded with a large smile, "I feel great."

"But your yard, it's…" she said, stopping her trail of words and motioning to the yellow dandelion field behind her.

"Beautiful."

"No Clive, it's not!" Owen shouted from the back of the crowd.

"And you can't go out looking like that," Megan added.

"There's nothing in the neighborhood charter saying I have to kill weeds, there's nothing that regulates how long my grass can be, and there certainly isn't anything in the charter about my facial hair," Clive said, confident that he had the upper hand and was acting within the charter's stipulations. Megan tried to bark out something, but Clive cut her off. "I've got every right to keep my lawn this way. And, as you can see, my trees are groomed, perfectly adhering to the guidelines set by the Liberty Lane Homeowners Association."

Clive pointed to the three Normal® trees. Megan, Owen, and the others turned to look. In the middle of the dandelions and grassy overgrowth, each tree was equidistant from the curb and the house, their lush leaves enveloping a meticulous, symmetrical frame. While everybody else's heads were turned, Clive slammed the door and went to sit in the warm glow beaming through his Customized™ window. People shouted at him through the glass, others pounded on the front door. Clive just smiled and clutched the old black and white photo, ignoring the mob.

The next day, Clive woke up to the dreaded hissing sound that he hadn't heard in over two months. He darted downstairs to make sure that his Yard Management System© was still disconnected. Indeed, everything was unplugged. Clive knew the malevolent hissing sound was coming from elsewhere, out on his lawn. He ran upstairs and tore open his front door. Three people in gray jumpsuits paced across Clive's lawn. They wore sinister black gas masks, and white tanks were strapped to their backs, snaking into gun-like hoses that rested in their writhing, gloved fingers. Clive covered his mouth and coughed as fumes wafted toward him. The dandelions and long stalks of unkempt grass withered in the dense chemical fog.

Clive ran outside and kicked the nearest toxician. The toxician struck back, but Clive's rage-addled mind ignored the pain. Clive tackled the toxician to the ground and straddled him. Clive ripped off the man's gas mask, throwing it into the nearby street. Clive landed two blows on the man's exposed face before the other two toxicians pulled him off. They held Clive down as he flailed his arms, screaming, tears streaking down his cheeks. A rough, gray first hit Clive's face. Blackness consumed Clive, but for a few moments he still heard the filtered, mechanical wheezing of the toxicians, even in the darkness.

Clive awoke to a bright light and a headache. "Good morning," a vaguely familiar voice said. Clive looked up to see the policeman who had ordered the tree trimming after Megan's complaint. The officer was behind a bright light in an otherwise dim room. His dark blue uniform sunk into the shadow, while his badge reflected light from the intense bulb.

"Where am I?"

The officer didn't answer. He just crossed his arms and glared at Clive.

"I had every right to let dandelions grow on my grass. You can't arrest me" Clive said, shielding his eyes from the bright light.

"Yes, you did have every right," the police officer remarked, "and the person who hired those toxicians is getting a hefty fine. But you didn't have any right to assault that man."

"He was killing my dandelions."

"They're just weeds," the officer said with a raised eyebrow.

The room shook. "Are we moving?" Clive asked, tightness rising in his chest.

"Yes," said the policeman. "We're in the back of a truck."

"Where are you taking me? Am I being deported?"

"No," the officer said, "but the Liberty Lane Homeowners Association has petitioned for you to be removed from the neighborhood. I have to honor their wishes."

"So where am I going?"

"None of the other neighborhoods in this area will take you. Word traveled fast about your little freak-out."

"So where the hell am I going?"

"The outskirts," the officer said. "From there you can hitch your way to some other community that might take you in. Worst case scenario, you can go to a city. Your credit card should still work, so you won't have a problem finding places to stay as you move across the country."

Clive had heard stories about the outskirts. He was told it was a wasteland where unpredictable danger lurked. In the outskirts, the only signs of civilization were the long stretches of old roadways that connected the region's various makeshift encampments. Before Clive could fully grapple with the severity of the situation, the truck ground to a stop.

"We're here," the officer said. "Take your time, make sure your head feels okay, then leave when you're ready. I slipped some painkillers in your pocket while you were out, in case that bruise gives you trouble later." The police officer exited through a door that connected to the truck's cabin. He latched the door behind him, leaving only the truck's exterior door unlocked for Clive's departure.

Clive sat alone in the bright light amid encroaching darkness. He pushed his shaking hand into the pocket of his flannel pajama pants. He rolled the plastic pill bottle over his fingers while his breaths grew shallow. He gripped the bottle in his hand and squeezed until he heard a pop. The bottle's flimsy lid flew off, and the tablets poured out from Clive's pocket, pitter-pattering across the truck's floor. Clive let go of the crushed bottle and reached for the door handle. He knew the sooner he exited the truck, the sooner he'd be back on his long trek toward civilization. He closed his eyes, sucked in a massive gulp of air, and yanked the door open. Clive's slipper-clad feet had barely touched the ground when the truck peeled away with the door still open. Clive opened his eyes and waved his hand through the air, trying to clear the dust.

When the haze settled, Clive collapsed to his knees. Tears of joy dropped from his eyes as he stared at the unbridled disorder before him. There were rolling hills, tall grasses, thick shrubs, and trees of all shapes and sizes. There was a gentle stream flowing through it all. Insects buzzed in the air. Leaves crisscrossed in and out of light and dark canopy spaces. Birds chirped, and squirrels scampered about. And throughout the entire sublime scene, peaking up from the mottled greenery, protruded thousands of bright yellow dandelions.

# MARS
Lance Nizami
Volume 2, Issue 2


Tell me, spaceman
When you walk that planet red and dusty dry
All jagged head-size rocks, and empty gullies
Where streams had run a billion years ago
What are your feelings

Can you among us know what really happened
Conceive of what was lost when slowly slowly
The planet's dynamo spun surely down

No force-field left of thin magnetic lines
To guide away the stinging solar wind
The oceans steamed away, escaped to space

Do you know now or can you tell
Or shed a single tear for something lost
Put one small mote of moisture back to soil
To see it hit that arid sponge, then fly,
Evaporate to pink transparent sky.

# DAYDREAM
Catherine Warren
Volume 2, Issue I


I would kiss you
through the screen
of my bedroom window

some summer night,
necks pricking
with summer sweat,

palms twinned, skin to
skin, searching lips
neatly gridded by wire.

I would cling to
your breath
if I could.

I hear the telephone.
I lick my lips and taste metal.

# TANDEM
Anna Wood
Volume I, Issue I

It's in moments like these, when she gives us both permission to act like the lie I've just told her is true, that I remember why I started saying the word "love" back to her in the first place, somewhere between eight and eighteen years ago. I'd just finished telling her that the reason I hadn't been in bed when she woke up this morning, today being the first Saturday she's had off in almost two months, was that I had had to get a last-minute breakfast with Max before he went on the air at quarter past ten. He needed another pep talk, I say. I make the same tired joke about the curse of being a cameraphobic newsman, and she gives the same tired smile she always does when she's in a tolerant-enough mood to politely acknowledge my punch line reruns.

"What was it this time? Bad haircut? Screwed the camera chick and never called back? Fearing on-air revenge?" Beth asks. She doesn't wait to hear the answer; she knows well enough one isn't coming.

It isn't that my alibi is unbelievable, exactly. There have been plenty of instances when my little brother has lost his shit at the most inopportune of moments, when I've been forced to go be the big sister, angel-of-comfort figure, leaving my girlfriend (whose tolerance is not always so steely as it appears to be on this day) to finish dinner alone, or run lines with no one but the dog for help, or take the tandem to work by herself because I need the car to get to Max. All we have is a two-seater car, an old Honda CRX, and a tandem. Sometime after the verbal *loveyou*s became reciprocal, we'd decided that wherever we ended up, we'd be going there together, and we wanted our vehicle purchases to reflect that fact. Neither of us really thought about how unpleasant riding the tandem solo would be, or how inconvenient it might be that we couldn't offer a friend a ride home. Neither of us had thought that kind of hypothetical was relevant.

So while Max's unpredictable crises—the only known antidote to which are the grounding advice sessions offered by his "queer mess of a big sister" (that being a quote from our uncle, orator extraordinaire and mayor of a small town not far enough away from here)—while they are frequent enough to serve as a plausible excuse, Beth's not having woken up when Max called to the ringing of my incredibly loud cell phone, or at the very least not having been woken up by me to say goodbye before I slipped out the door, were facts compelling enough to make her feel certain that, whatever it is I was doing this morning, it had little to do with helping out a brother in need. I know she knows this, and she knows I know she knows this. But it's sunny outside for the first time in a long time, and it's her day off.

"Are you hungry?" I ask. "I can make you some eggs."

"Samantha." A full sentence. "I'm at this moment bleeding profusely onto a wad of cotton shoved up my vagina. Don't mention the word *egg*."

"English muffin?" This also happens to be one of my pet names for her. I think myself charming.

"You know that tonight's opening night. I have to focus," she says, walking by me and out the back door. I hear her plunk down the steps to the concrete courtyard of our apartment complex, fully equipped with giant urns apparently designed to hold decorative plants. Probably miniature palm trees. In the three years we've been here the plants have failed to appear, though Beth continues to hold out hope. The sound of her flicking a lighter repeatedly carries through the still-open door; I can almost feel the vibrations of her trembling hands. Nervous or angry or just in need of a fix?

I vaguely consider pointing out to the now-empty kitchen that the use of the term "opening night" for a show that's set only to run three times, one of which will be the Sunday matinee (half price for seniors and students, free for the lucky ones screwing the stars), was a bit disingenuous. Though part of me is grateful for the fragile peace that we're operating under, another part of me seems to still want the fight that hasn't yet materialized. This latter is probably the same part of me that had been getting psyched up about the impending altercation on the drive back home, thinking of what she'd say and what I'd say and how I'd win, ultimately, simply because I have more invested in the outcome. I bite my lower lip and brush some crumbs left over from yesterday's midnight feast of breadsticks and marinara sauce off the kitchen counter and onto the linoleum floor. I watch the crumbs lands in almost perfect irregularity, note that they've got plenty of company down there, and turn on the upper-left stove burner, upon which sits a new but decidedly not new-looking kettle. I would make her tea, she would consider me repentant, and the unspoken distrust and anger and hurt would be swept out of sight temporarily, just so many crumbs of fourth-rate Italian food.

Beth not only thinks she knows where I wasn't—at breakfast with Max—she also thinks she's got a pretty good idea about where I was. This, she does not know I know. She likes to think the tabs she keeps on me are subtle enough that I don't notice. I haven't been able to break it to her that anyone who does glorified community theater in Pensacola, Florida, still dreams about her big break at the no-longer-tender age of 29 and genuinely *cries* while bowing at the end of a show is incapable of being subtle about anything. Least of all about alleged secrets kept by her girlfriend, partner, lover. I don't like any of those words, nor do I particularly care for the word "secret," if only because it implies that privacy is somehow damnable. It happens to be, for the very same reason, one of Beth's favorites. She once suggested that we keep a shared journal, that together we compose memories of various nonevents, together we articulate our pressing concerns (assumed to be mutual) about the past, present, future. I made the mistake then of merely laughing at the idea, which she took as enough of a vote of support to go out and actually buy a notebook.

"You first," Beth had said that night, gesturing with her tiny, pointy nose, her only truly prize-winning feature, to the notebook. She had set it, a huge, red, leather-bound monstrosity, atop the coffee table when she came home from rehearsal. Next to it were her sunglasses and keys. I found myself wondering what kind of animal has red skin, realizing that underneath its fur a creature could be any color at all. I liked the idea. Beth was busy painting her toenails a navyish color, one of my old bandanas tied around her head to keep her hair out of her eyes as she curled over herself, cat-like, to apply thick, even strokes of polish onto her slightly yellowed nails. She is a master at such minor arts.

"Can I write about how alluring you look wearing that bandana?" I asked. "Like some little Eastern European vagrant, beautiful and damned?"

She tried to keep herself from smiling at that. This is what she does instead of laughing, ever fearful of the evaporation of dignity that goes hand-in-hand with her still girlish giggle. "Selling matches on a cold winter's night?" she parried, lips cautiously neutral.

"The little match girl was French," I responded. Incorrectly, as it happens. "Your roots are showing, rube."

This failed to provoke another careful non-smile from her. She was genuinely offended, dove into one of her theatrical rages to which I periodically become spectator, never able to be sure what she sincerely thinks or feels because her actual emotions are as overblown as any of the ones she learns from scripts. No one but Beth, I think, experiences Rage the way it's imagined by playwrights, or Joy or Fear or Love or any of the rest of them. Doctors talk about "textbook cases" of various frightening illnesses; according to that same logic, Beth is a screenplay case.

Beth, the aspiring actress, Beth the belle of Panhandle theater, Beth the Unsubtle, does not like the word "rube," nor does she like references to her roots. And not in the way that any non-New Yorker or new money type doesn't like references to their roots; this goes much deeper. Something about Beth that she would rather people didn't know: She has never been out of the country. Has never left the southeastern quadrant of the United States, with the one exception of a life-defining weekend in New York City at the age of eleven. (Every subsequent day of her life has been compared to those thirty-seven hours, and not one of them has come out ahead.) Another unmentionable: Beth never finished college, even, not that the one she started at was anything impressive to begin with. She had made the big move from the suburbs of Jacksonville to Tallahassee to go to TCC, with the ultimate plan of transferring to FSU. But, as with so many Florida kids with that fine dream, Beth eventually decided that the minimal effort necessary to transfer to Florida State wasn't worth it, particularly when visits to local parties and bars revealed the fact that there was no substantive difference (let alone higher IQ average) between the community college kids and the state college kids. Their Wednesday-morning hangovers were equally unpleasant and equally predictable. It was only one step further for her to determine (once more in sizeable, if not good, company) that there was also no substantive difference between the college-educated and the non-, a determination that led her once more to start life afresh a few dozen miles to the west, this time hitching a ride from Tallahassee to join me in Pensacola. She's been here ever since.

I have an excuse for being here, at least, as does Max. Our dad was Navy. Hence Pensacola to begin with. He left his third wife for a younger woman who later left him, and then he developed Alzheimer's and needed someone to take care of him. Hence Pensacola for me. And Max can't function without me, even without a diagnosis to justify it. Hence Pensacola for him. My roots are less funny, if equally miserable.

This is not the kind of town where it takes much time to feel like you know the place, know it really well. Beth talks about specials at the Winn-Dixie and changes on the menus of the local diners like a local, perceiving even the minutest of shifts in description of how, exactly, the eggs are prepared or from whence the citrus this year came. This is not something I mention to her, either, the fact that she speaks of pork specials in the precise dialect of my high school friends' grandmothers. But, superficial impressions aside, there's a lot to be known about the town that can't exactly be taught, cultural knowledge that is only earned with time (ill-)spent here. This is another fact I choose not to discuss with Beth. It's a difficult balancing act with her, as she's just as ready to be offended by the accusation of *outsider* as of *native*.

So Beth feels she has a pretty good idea of where I was this morning because she feels she has a pretty good idea of the potential places I have to go. At the top of that short list is surely Chuck's, which never closes, even if Chuck isn't actually watching the place, even if he's collapsed in the back, sleeping. During those hours people just pour themselves their own drinks, try their best to keep the coffee fresh and bottles corked, or at least upright, and leave behind various sums of money calculated in mysterious ways before stumbling out into society once more. The money is traditionally left in whatever location seems inoffensively close at hand, not requiring much standing or lurching or stretching; Chuck passes the slower hours wandering about the place, looking between cushions, underneath ash heaps and inside half-filled glasses for the quarters and dimes that apparently add up to a rent-worthy sum. The addictive thing about Chuck's is that as soon as you walk out, the whole world seems suffocatingly judgmental, out to tell you how you've most recently fucked up, how this time it's really irreparable, this time you've really done it, this time you've really, this time you've, this time. You start remembering Chuck's as the one place that isn't *that*. And the longer you're out in the real world, the more appealing Chuck's starts to seem, so in addition to the three or four regulars who enviably inhabit this utopia full-time, there's a steady stream of customers who come in on staggered schedules, some X weeks/days/hours/lays since their last visit, like sick clockwork, in need of reprieve once more. I've seen the Baptist teetotalers, on break from distributing flyers and Cokes outside liquor stores, nursing bottles at Chuck's more than once. Given the spirit of the place, though, this is not something that's mentioned. Ever. This is the kind of thing Beth doesn't know about Pensacola. And obviously not the kind of thing I would be able to explain.

If Beth pictures my early morning hours spent at Chuck's, which she well might, her theory as to what specifically drove me to the liquid embrace of neutrality is something I can't guess. Not that there's nothing she or I could think of—more that there's too much, and too much too consistently, for me to be able to think of one reason that stands out more than others. In all likelihood, she feels the same way and has not stopped to examine whether recent events with my father, or lack of work, or fights with her, or nostalgia for the few years of my life I had imagined myself free of this place, or maybe even whether it was the dog's incessant barking that drove me out of our home sometime between two and seven this morning. None of these cues would alter her lines. She probably knows this. She may even be able to guess that I know that she, in all likelihood, knows this.

Jen would have had a specific idea. Jen always had specific, if flawed, ideas. She also would have exploded when I walked in the door a few minutes before eleven. Accusations of seeing my ex, sleeping with my ex, wanting to leave her for my ex would have come flying. And if I hadn't supposedly been to Chuck's with that ex just a few minutes prior, this fight would have been more than enough to drive me there. But it was Jen, of all people, who got out of here, ran away to Ohio with some boy who had dreams of fields filled with wheat, leaving me puzzled as to which part of that story was more bizarre, the boy or the fantasy. But it's hard to mock her for long. It's me who's still here, and I've never even seen wheat fields. They might be nice.

There are some things I have seen. I've seen the inside of libraries. I've seen the inside of what must be the nicest library south of the Mason-Dixon. Back when I was at Chapel Hill, back when I thought the trajectory of my life was assuredly upward-bound, meaning northbound away from Florida, I spent hours in the various libraries, Law, Engineering, Health, just trying to take in the fact that there were so many buildings full of books waiting to be read. For free. In shock at the fact that so many spines cracked when you flipped open the books, brand-new, never-before-read. How could a perfectly good book be so utterly neglected? My favorite library was the Wilson, where the university kept its rare books, including room upon room dedicated to William Butler Yeats, full of scripts he'd scribbled all over, books he'd written and later wanted destroyed, letters. Yeats was a patriot and member of the Eugenics Society. The handicapped are ruining our species by having too many babies. Being queer isn't so bad; we don't tend to breed. There's a lot you can learn in a library.

The water is boiling. There are no clean mugs left, so I wash one quickly, swirling around the soap suds with my hand because I'm pretty sure the sponge contains so many months of bacteria it just makes our dishes dirtier. I have equally little confidence in the dish towel wedged behind the handle on the refrigerator door and wipe the mug dry on my shirt. I'm wearing my green flannel shirt, the one Beth loves. The one that brings out my eyes. Beth drinks Lipton Yellow Label tea, half a dozen or so cups a day. She used to be ashamed that she didn't enjoy the taste of coffee, as it seemed in her measure an essential component of not just an actress' but any sort of sophisticated person's identity. She admitted this pretty early on in our relationship, and I pointed out that it made her different, interesting. The second adjective went over better than the first, a fact that I recorded and made use of later. Once she began taking pride in her tea-drinking, I found myself unable to point out that tea snobbery hardly implies Lipton.

I pour the boiling water over the tea bag, watch the cup cloud up with color and open the refrigerator. No milk. Perhaps she won't take this gesture as a sign of repentance, after all. She comes in now, smelling of cigarettes and calmer, nods in the general direction of the tea.

"Thanks."

"You look like you could use it."

She opens the refrigerator. No milk. She sighs and stirs a few spoonfuls of sugar into the mug. She does not wash the spoon beforehand. I'm good to her, I think. I do not say this, either. She takes her mug into the bedroom. I hear her set it down on a wooden surface, probably the bedside table, and then I hear the television. Static. Then news. Local news, meaning car crashes, weather and arrests. They do not say those arrested are black, but I know they are. The anchors know I know they are. Something else I couldn't explain to Beth.

"Fuck," she says. I cringe. "Fuck, fuck, fuck."

This is my cue. "What's wrong, Beth?"

"I can't find my tights. I specifically put them on top of the dresser last night so that I wouldn't freak out looking for them today. Now I can't fucking find them."

"Did you look on the floor?"

"What am I, a retard? Not everyone is as dysfunctional as your little brother, Sam. God *damn* it."

There is no reasonable response I can give. Nor is there any way for me to remain silent this time. Not saying anything will not redeem this situation. There will be a fight. She will be in tears, after being merely enraged, after more likely than not throwing something sharp or heavy at me, after accusing me of all sorts of disloyalties, after telling me she can't stand the sight of me. Whether I tell her to look in her purse or offer to go buy her a new pair at WalMart, I am fated to hear her tell me she no longer loves me, that she doesn't want anything to do with me anymore, that she never needed me to begin with. Her lines are set. Mine are interchangeable.

I sigh and turn off the stove. I had forgotten, and the underside of the kettle is undoubtedly burnt. If I end up going to get her new tights, I will pick up a new tea kettle, as well.

What Beth doesn't know about me, what Beth doesn't know about this morning, is huge. It's one of very few things I would really like to explain to her, actually, if I thought it were possible. I really would like to tell her that I woke up at 4:30 this morning in a panic, barely able to breathe, that I woke up feeling I'd be unable to get through another day, a full day with her and my father and the dog, and that I slipped silently out of bed, too frightened to cry. I'd like to tell her about reaching for the dresser in the dark, picking out clothes by feel, searching especially for my soft flannel shirt, knowing even in that moment that it would make her forgive my absence more readily once I returned, then crawling on the floor in search of my sandals and shutting the door behind me as silently as possible. I would like to tell her what driving there was like, down those roads I had taken every Sunday as a child but never actually driven myself, guiding myself via nothing more than muscle memory to Second Coming Methodist Church. I would like to tell her what a horrifying feeling it was to see the Jesus carving on the wall standing just at eye-level, when all my memories of him involve looking upwards, northwards, reverent. How unnerving it was that he was on the same plane as I was, looking at me like he'd been waiting, looking at me like a friend. How that made me scared, before I even entered the building, that he wasn't strong enough to save me. I'd like to tell her about pushing open the side door, the one that never locks, about walking down the hall to the chapel. I'd like to describe to her the way the pews looked too empty, too far away, too lonely for me to approach. I'd like to tell her, after a pause, that I went to the pulpit instead, leaned my back against the cold wood, and that from that perspective Jesus was high up again, way up on the wall, larger than me, larger than life, looking away from me, dying for me.

I'd like to tell Beth, if I could, how I prayed for the first time since I was twenty-one and pulled out of college three months before graduation, dragged back to Pensacola by my father whose brain cells are dissolving day by day. I would tell her, if the words existed, that it was my first time in this church since my mother died, leaving me, ten, to watch out for Max, six. I'd like to tell her what I prayed for. That after staring at Jesus for several minutes, after looking upwards til my neck began to ache, I began praying for patience. Patience. I couldn't even get myself to pray for an escape from this place, from these people, pray to be free of it all. I just prayed for patience to go back home, to be good to the woman I say *love* to, even if I should really be saying it to a man (I prayed for forgiveness for a moment, too). For patience to watch my father forget me, for patience to stand by as my beautiful brother gradually compromises away his dreams. I'd like to tell all this to Beth, if she'd listen, but I know I can't, I know it's not in her script.

I take a deep breath. "Have you looked in your purse?" I ask.

# Aftermath

Elyse Brownell
Volume I, Issue 4


And so what if I shared all my secrets
with a man I barely know,
on a first date, under the bar lights,
under the light of a future I thought I could have,
with this man I barely know.

It's a time or two similar to these
where we regret to have finally opened up,
to have bared our chest on the countertops,
when it would have been
an easier task and much more rewarding,
had I unbuttoned my blouse to a man I do know,
and I tried to know, but couldn't quite crack through the surface,
nor allow the foam to settle before taking it all back in
one gulp.

And so what if I was emotionally slutty,
in front of this man I barely know,
and dug deep inside myself,
to pull out only the good qualities that I possess
and dangle them in front of him,
like car keys to a child.

I may have supported Ted Bundy's motives
because he did, because he defends bottom-dwellers,
and all that matters is whether or not

there is probable cause,
whether or not it's beyond a reasonable doubt,
whether or not your soul comes out that day,
or stays tucked away still.

And maybe I talked a little bit too much about humanity,
about basic human rights,
"sex is a basic human right," he said.
I should have left then, but I laughed and said
"not as easily attainable to all," scanning the room,
pointing out the misfortunes who probably have more
sex than Bukowski (who was hideous),
and don't write about it or flaunt it, but accept it
as a daily routine, as something as necessary as breakfast,
or a first mug of dark roast.

Maybe it was my secrets that made him stray,
unfaithful before midnight,
under the bar lights watching my future
play back in films on countertops.
Or the exposure of myself, reflecting in his,
realizing I haven't stood with both feet
on firm ground in quite some time.

# SOLACE WITHIN THE SHADOWS:
## The Power of Memoir
Sheila Hageman
Volume 2, Issue I

I remember the day I discovered the power of memoir. It hit me in a rush of red maples that grew along 75th Street in Jackson heights, NY, where I lived. It was mid-afternoon in late summer before I began graduate school for my MFA in creative writing.

I was obsessively worrying about my mother who was ill with breast cancer as I pushed my daughter Genny in her stroller; I stopped to pick up a dropped baby doll and happened to look up. There the blossoming trees hovered above me, but they were not just trees, they were magic transporters back to my childhood, back to my green, suburban lawn, back to another time of life when my family was all together and healthy.

How accustomed I had become to rushing through life without stopping and looking around me. I had so much responsibility and worry. I did not even know what I was missing in my daily life—from simply enjoying the beauty of nature around me to the treasures of deeper reflections about my past that could be triggered by my physical surroundings.

When my sister and I were born, my grandfather planted us each a sapling in our backyard; my tree had grown into a magnificent red maple and Peggy's green maple towered just above it. That tree was mine; it was me. As it grew, so did I. And it was always there, sturdy and strong, surrounded by backyard blue sky when I looked up.

Surrounded by that same blue sky as I knelt on the sidewalk, I felt hyperaware of my place in the world and time, but with a cry from Genny, I shook off my musings, stood up, and pushed back into the mind-numbing tedium of new motherhood.

This awareness of our present moments can launch us into the stories of our pasts at unexpected moments, but the technique can also be harvested, practiced, and used as we set out to consciously discover memories. The intertwined beauty of beginning our stories from where we are, from what we are doing, and then delving into the recollections and places these triggers can take us, is the special reward memoir affords us as writers.

Remembering my tree meant remembering playing kickball—the garbage can was always first base, Peggy's tree was second base, and my red maple was third. Home base was different things all the time, but our trees always remained the same. We would play until we were sweaty and grass-stained and my mother's voice would echo from the screened-in back porch: "Peggy! Sheila! Dinner!"

We would run inside, leaving the shade and protection behind us. And to remember that time is to remember my mother and all our wholeness even as we were mired in our myriad dysfunctions.

Even though we'd all moved away, I found comfort in knowing our trees still stood as I looked up at my Queens, NY, trees. I could feel it deep within. The sap that flowed through my childhood tree flowed through every red maple and through me.

As I began my graduate study of memoir I became even more alert to the world around me, to the people in my immediate sight and experience, and I used the things and people I saw in a whole new way (and I mean "used" in a totally healthy way, of course!).

I had been working on my memoir for ten years, thinking it was a coming-of-age story about how I had become a stripper. I had lines in my proposal like: My stilettos stepped tentatively onto a stage with spilled beer slithering through the cracks. For every bill that I clutched in my hand, another word was scribbled into my journal, where I tried to make sense of what I was witnessing, feeling, and becoming. I take you with me along the naked path I walked through the inspirational struggle of a girl becoming a woman in these very complicated years at the end of the Twentieth Century.

There was nothing inherently bad or wrong about what I had written so far. It was a straight forward story of a period of my life, an exploration of what I had experienced and learned. I'm thankful now that no publisher grabbed up my first attempt. There was something missing from my story; I discovered what when I stopped only looking at my past and began to get more aware of the present and more associative in my thinking.

As I brainstormed ideas in my memoir workshops, I found I was focused on all the trials and tribulations of the present—my mother's illness and my own experience of being a new mother to a daughter. As I allowed myself to delve into my present day experiences I soon found a new window, a new angle of seeing what I had previously only seen in a surface way. Suddenly, my writing became more layered and intriguing not only to me, but to my readers.

By beginning in the present, but not staying there, I was able to discover new layers of meaning to my past experience. Having been a stripper was no longer a closed-off and singular experience, now there was an exploration of what my present experiences as a mother and a daughter had to do with my past. There were rich undertones of mother-daughter issues, body images, and illness and health in the female form.

Though I have now lost my mother, I have regained something of her by writing my memoir. I made a record of those days that I spent adrift in loss. The process of my mother's dying forced upon me a kind of vision, a looking inward which was a gift at that horrible time. Through being present to my reality at the time, I was able to understand more deeply the meanings of my past experiences.

I was able to view, to experience, the decline of the female form in the present and explore what it was to have a female body. I felt the stigmas and desires and definitions we make through our bodies. I witnessed the illnesses of our society as represented in female form—physical and mental illness. I was able to examine more deeply the meanings that lie within the breasts. The body. How we hide ourselves by hiding our bodies. How our bodies express what we can't, either through illness or through joy. And through grief.

Like the grief my stepfather Marc experienced after my mother's death. I remember visiting Marc for the last time before he moved to Texas. We ate pizza with him at Paradise Pizza in Stratford. I could not tell his secret, but I feel like I should have seen the signs within his slumped body, his hollow eyes. He was drinking again.

Afterwards, we drove by my childhood house in Trumbull. There was a new shed in back. The pricker bush still sat atop the driveway. Two cars were parked in the driveway just like Mom and Dad used to. Close, but not touching.

And there, my red maple lifted above the house to see. As if standing on tiptoe to let me know it was still there. Still strong.

My husband Nick said, "Go knock on the door."

But I was not so bold, or maybe I didn't really want to see the changes on the inside. I wasn't ready to see the change up close. I was still in the circling-around phase. Maybe I'll write a letter to the owners of the house one day. Stop back without Genny. Just like I've always wanted to stop back at The Hideaway, the first strip club I ever danced in.

I wonder if I'll ever actually do it. Step back inside. Go back and visit a world that's closed to me now.

The first time I stripped: Stamford, CT; Industrial Park; buildings; roads and trucks; Madonna. The first President George Bush. Entering the Persian Gulf War. Should I be going there? Be doing something important with my life. I had just graduated high school. A feeling of there being an in-between time. Anti-war sentiment rising amongst youth—my wishing I could be part of it. What did I think I couldn't be? I'd already boxed myself in…to youth and beauty and desire. A reverting to 60's fashion. More free in clothes. Was it grunge time yet? A freedom to be who you were that didn't exist in the 80's while I was in high school. A feeling that I'd been born too early or too late. I was always too young or too old.

The immediate environment: from sun, warmth, to dark coolness. A darkness that sucked the life of the sun out. Cold air. Damp smell. Emptiness. Before customers arrived—it was just an empty shell of place, not what it really was. An empty bar. Base lights. A stark stage. Cheap looking. Crass. The skeletons of a fantasy world, behind the scenes. No beauty. Plain walls, bar, stools, stark folding metal chairs pushed haphazardly around bland L-shaped stage. Ugliness. Pool tables like coffins waiting to be lowered into the ground. Then, when the lights came on. I'd forgotten it was day out. Time ceased to exist.

I wonder if it's still the same owner. Or if the same bartender still tells his junkie monkey story from Vietnam. Or if there's still a cooler at the back of the bar with saran-wrapped ham and cheese sandwiches for lunch.

Or if anyone would still remember my name if I walked in the door with my duffel bag slung casually across my shoulder.

Even as I write now, I witness the choppiness of my life and how I remember experiences; I cannot write without this associative meandering. I made the choppiness a part of the structure of my memoir throughout. To help the reader understand what my experience of life as a woman is like.

How do I convey to you a story lived in the flesh? How do I show the body's experience in words?

If I want you to know what it feels like to stand naked onstage— to feel vulnerable, ugly, alone, scared, wanted, desired, hated, sworn at, hit on, cold with hard nipples, beautiful, perfect, flawed, unloved, lusted after, rejected—then I must show you a fractured life, one that has no beginning or end in present or past, but a life that flows and sways much as I find my body doing today as a mother rocking my child, to the days I held my mother's weak hand and squeezed, to the days I sold the erotic dances my body could create, and to the early days when my body simply rolled in the green grass below my blooming maple's shadow.

# SPILLING
Jennifer Brennock
Volume I, Issue 3

On Monday, there were two lines on the pee stick. Tuesday, there was only one. I added the stick with two lines to my collection and threw away the other. On Wednesday, I got on a plane.

I'm tightly seated on a jumbo jet, requisite lap belt affixed. Preventing my body from spilling out of my allotted space feels like a test I will surely fail. But I'm already spilling. I've been quietly losing large quantities of blood and a tiny, failed life since take-off three hours ago.

I had to steal the pad I'm filling now from the airport bathroom before the flight because I was armed with only one lint-covered o.b. and was out of quarters. While being reminded not to miscarry someone else's baggage by the automated p.a., I worked a flattened fist wrist-deep up the dispenser hole, just barely snagging the pink plastic edge with an awkward twist of fingers, me performing a pelvic instead of receiving one. I thanked whichever goddess was in charge of feminine hygiene machines and figured four would be enough.

On the plane, I'm filling the fourth to capacity. There is something nervy and hot tugging on my uterus like a dental tool. The feeling reminds me of a street performer using his nipple rings to suspend himself above ground. I shift in the seat. I glance peripherally at my seatmates, who are already annoyed. An elderly woman to my right and a man to my left. Neither have what I need.

The plane is flying in the exact opposite direction of my home. It's going to Connecticut, a place where the only people I know are a gaggle of women I have met only once. They are the women my husband came from, women who lunch, who admire each other's mink jackets and blood diamonds, who don't mention the words uterus or menses, and only occasionally concede to say "down there" in a whisper. My husband stayed behind. A meeting came up. He'll follow on Saturday.

As I spill, the human sounds claiming every square inch of the aircraft are at once too loud and too distant, as if I'm being held under water and there is a raging party just above the surface. The riotous distribution of salty snacks and plastic cups of gin are passed like shining toys emerging from Santa's sack. I shake my head when she asks me the same question she's been asking for the fifteen rows in front of me, the same question she will continue to ask for the interminable rows behind. Her lips look as if she has dipped them perfectly into a pool of new blood. I shift in the seat. Two more hours seems like a very long time. I feel hot and sticky between my legs as I check the seat pocket for my barf bag. I pull it out to keep it handy. It looks too small. It's a joke. It's a gag gift.

My morbid thoughts shame me, but I can't help wishing I could watch the blood drip, to witness its flight from my body, a last look at my runaway child. I want to quantify the amount, to record its length and weight. I'm disappointed I can't see the exact hue. Would the color have dimension, like a ruby on a fluttering hand, or would it be opaque like a cherry skin? The pad is heavy. I know it can't go on like this.

Seconds after I push the overhead button with its tiny, symbolic flight attendant, the real one looms above me, her lipstick so glossy it may spill too. With a junior high smile I ask if she has any feminine hygiene products aboard. She recoils and says "I'm sorry" as if she has been manufactured not to need those things, as if only the arcane need tampons and pads.

I tell her, "I really, really need one. I'm having kind of a problem." "What kind of *problem*?"

All I can think to tell her, and my seatmates who are politely pretending not to hear, is I'm having a miscarriage. I'm losing a lot of blood. I didn't come prepared. It was the wrong thing to say.

Quickly she is in action. She cannot be slowed. She touches my leg. She calls me "Dear." Then she is on the p.a. "Is there a doctor on board?" I'm shaking my head, but she doesn't see me. She doesn't know I'm a veteran, that this is nearly routine. How do I say to her and her perfect lapels, "Hey, it happens all the time. No biggee. Hey, don't worry about it. I don't." Anymore.

There is a doctor on board. She's a pediatrician. The irony makes me hide a smirk. The man next to me is asked to move from his seat. As he gathers up his belongings, I apologize, and he gives me a look of fright that makes me more nauseous. The doctor takes his seat. She also calls me "Dear." She asks me a few questions and I treat them with the seriousness she expects. I don't want her to think I am unaware of my body, that I can't control its functions. I remind myself I'm powerful. I took back the night years ago. I'm a force of reckoning. I will not be fucked with. She's saying she has the power to take the plane down for an emergency landing right this very minute. Her face wears a strange excitement as if she's about to bite into a very rare steak, blood rare. She's horny for her own exercise of power.

"I just need another pad."

The man in the next aisle is sipping red wine. It's a dark, cherry skin color. I don't mention to the doctor that I need a drink the size of my head and a couple valium too if she's packing. She tells me it's not as simple as a pad and I need to be seen by a medical professional as soon as possible. I'm smart enough to know now is not the time to tell her I don't believe in Western medicine and her entire profession is in my mind the only thing we capitalists purchase before we see the price tag.

The doctor and the stewardess converse without my input. I am moved to an empty seat in first class because it's closer to the door. When we layover in Detroit, I will be the first off the plane. An incontinence diaper is found. When I put it on in the cell-like lavatory, I put my soaked underwear in the trash hiding them beneath discarded paper towels. A stream of blood—a hue I hadn't thought of, the charity pink of a grandma's couch—runs down my inner thigh and I catch it midstream with the t.p. I want to put the blood-soaked paper in my pocket. We all save mementos of our lost loves. Instead I let it go down with the rest, sucked dry and violently into the plane's innards, because it is what it is—human waste.

When the plane door is opened, there are three paramedics

with badges and a stretcher on the other side as attentive as war. I tell them I don't need it; I can walk just fine. They say I have to. The word policy is uttered. I look down the bustling concourse and wonder if I should run.

I like one of the paramedics despite his patronizing smile. He's a huge man but there is an infant gentleness about him that reminds me of someone whose feelings are hurt easily. His name is Glen or something. He helps me up on the thing. He straps me down with a system of three point restraints. Glen brushes fallen hair from my forehead with clumsy fingers. I think Glen is still a little scared of women.

"I'm not going to let anything happen to you," he tells me.

But "anything" has already happened, and I'm immediately impaled by his lie. It guts me through like a newly-dead fish, and I can no longer keep my innards in their proper places. I'm quickly sobbing ugly. I am two people. One loose and raw, strapped down like a mental patient, a danger to herself, in need of collection and proper disposal. The other is a Mother Superior standing above myself, judging the woman who is so clearly losing her shit, and telling her that she deserves this shame. I am both lost and self-righteous as, like a funeral procession, the stretcher leads from the plane the line of passengers who are respectfully quiet but anxious to get by and make their connections. They all know about me now. They all know I can't do what every other woman on the planet seems to naturally. The blood spilling from me might as well cover my entire body and mark me. A rain of cherry skins and rubies, red lipstick tubes and pomegranates to paint me with. The crimson of a matador's cape soaked into every pore. I remember my red anniversary panties, and I throw up a little. I let it fall into my hand from the height of my mouth because my arms are held by the safety policy and my elbows can no longer bend.

The stretcher railroads down the concourse to a service elevator. Glen inserts his special key. He looks at me indirectly and tells me the hospital is not far away. He says it like we're on a date, like he's taking me out for ice cream. I watch the numbers— four, three, two, one—fall from their own tiny heights. One by one, their red lives are extinguished. I picture my mother-in-law fur-clad and stood up at the Hartford airport. She's always known I'm not good enough for her son and today she's finally right.

The elevator doors open to the tarmac and a barren wind. The ambulance is parked not far away, angled for a quick getaway, red lights orbiting silently. I tell Glen to wait and he obeys my command like a boy in love. I look down at the straps and back to his dimpled face. I beg him with my eyes.

"Please? Just to your bus?"

He unbuckles me, but he doesn't like it. Once I'm standing, Glen has his arm around my waist. For a moment, I want to dance with him, a little trip across the tarmac, light as air, encircled in his arms. I imagine a flowing white dress and a Sinatra tune about flying away and the feeling of Glen's forearm under my palm. I want to move against him with the rhythm of a rocking chair while the serious workers wearing their ear protection and driving the mysterious hydraulic machines pass us by. The jet engines are roaring against a Detroit February and all I want is to lay my head to final rest on Glen's enormous chest, to hear the unfailing beat of his ox-sized heart, to let myself melt all over him, because I am wasted now. I want him to lead me in a waltz where the music is only imagined and our steps go nowhere while the ambulance drives away and leaves us alone. I want him to tell me I don't have to go to the hospital, that I've been forgiven and he won't let anyone judge me. "You're just a child yourself," he'd say. "We all are." I'd close my eyes and tell him he's a wonderful dancer because he's the kind of man who needs compliments.

The ambulance doors are opened. I'm supposed to climb in after the stretcher is loaded. But I don't want to leave the weather-tormented tarmac. What's the point? It's all been lost already. Everything inside me has been emptied, and there is nowhere I need to be right now. I have nothing left to spill. Glen waits for me to take a step, but he doesn't tell me I have to.

On Monday, there were two lines on the pee stick. On Tuesday, there was only one.

# SHORE
Jade Leone Blackwater
Volume I, Issue 3


Here are the words which are hard to find:
Silurian
Sirenian
Serenity.

Toes express
indigo, tidal steps,
infinite synonyms
for fortitude.

Hear wind chime vowels grow
in the heart of the ear,
ankles frothed and anchored,
taste the dawn salarium.

Calyx,
quivering shell,
receive liquid moonlight,
be filled and stilled.

# ON COMMONPLACE AILMENTS
Sarah Lucille Marchant
Volume I, Issue 4

The giraffe carries his words like piano intestines. "It is my art," he often threatens in a voice that sounds nice.

He stops by the tailor's shop on his way to take his afternoon coffee because he needs a new button for his coat. "Those shoes in the window," he comments, "would look better with laces a shade or two darker."

The tailor takes a breath, considers his reply, but is unable to speak. The sensation in his throat is not unlike that of just-tuned cello strings, being plucked one by one.

In the town's only coffee house, the giraffe slurps up his mocha-whipped cream and chocolate sauce drizzled on—beside the butcher and the baker. "What have you slaughtered today?" the baker inquires.

"A wee chicken the neighbors brought," the butcher laments. He takes his time stirring his black tea. "What have you baked today?"

"A loaf of bread, a pan of brownies," the baker remarks. He sips his coffee and continues. "Should make quite the treat for little Tammy's birthday supper." After another small sip, he mutters "needs a bit more cream" to no one in particular.

"Well I," the giraffe begins without prompting, "perused a volume of Cummings'—could hardly be considered his best—as well as a few of Shakespeare's sonnets. The form nourished the Muse within me, you see, so I set out to write a sonnet of my own—all in honor of my little octopus. Wouldn't you know, the dear persists in believing that she's too ill to be bothered, so I placed it upon her bedside table. In my opinion, an ailment as commonplace as a cold is hardly reason to waste days inside and under blankets—and her cough's as infrequent as ever."

"I do enjoy Shakespeare," the butcher replies softly, sprinkling sugar into his cup.

"Do you think a fresh loaf of bread would improve her condition?" the baker asks.

"Don't worry yourselves, gentlemen. The little darling only desires attention—I'm sure that her good health is yet perfectly intact. All the same, she requested I return home before the evening falls, so I suppose I should be on my way."

"Send your wife my best wishes for a swift recovery," the butcher tells him.

"If you change your mind, my shop is open until seven," the baker reminds him.

The giraffe bestows his "goodbye" and their words flutter aside, limp leaves in a summer storm.

The giraffe tugs his plaid scarf tighter and bemoans his spots.

# FLIGHT
James Fowler
Volume I, Issue 4

His roving eye spotted her as he was downing a rib plate. Though she was posed like the other girls in a cottony, loose-fitting dress, something in her stance and expression refused to blend in with the group, arranged in rows by sex in front of the school building. The boys were all in jackets and ties, with their hair slicked back and parted in that once jazzy style. Most looked serious, as this was the age before smiling was allowed in group shots, but a couple guys down front seemed to be smirking at least. These would have been his friends. And they would have been the only ones with a chance at that girl he was seventy-five years too late for.

A few of the other girls sported similar, boyish cuts, but she wore it best. On them it was a fashion copied from a woman's magazine; on her it was a silky frame for a face that must have had many looks, the majority of them rebellious. He was sure she smoked and drank, even though the county was dry back then too. She would be the type to keep a small silver flask hidden on her. Once the borrowed Model-T was parked under some trees, she would produce it, take a swig, and offer some very casual-like. Her eyes would gleam in the dark. Even in the photo they were a focal point, at least for him. He guessed they were a light grey, clear with a frank kind of knowing.

"Hey Cole, see something you like?"

Jimmy was grinning through his toothpick. Ty and Lester paused in their talk about bass, expecting to see a live one walking by, then waited on Jimmy for the follow-through. He scanned the photo but couldn't pick the object of Cole's interest from the lineup. And Cole wasn't about to give him any help. Jimmy was one of those guys who could poke a hole in you once he found a soft spot.

"What I like is a classic truck that ain't filled with crappy country lite."

Ty and Lester hooted, starting in on Jimmy's music tastes. While he was still the new guy on the job after some months, Cole felt comfortable enough to do his own jabbing. He had been accepted pretty quickly, being a hometown boy and all, a familiar type. Sometimes his mouth or attitude raised hackles, but not enough to get him fired. Actually, if he timed it right, he stood a chance of getting laid off just as he was coming eligible for unemployment comp. Then all he would have to do is pretend to look for work and enjoy a paid vacation. He figured he had earned it after all that time absorbing glue fumes. The hot face mask and goggles didn't stop the stuff from getting into his skin. Denise said making love with him was like putting model planes together. As a teen he would have thought it a great deal to get seven dollars an hour to sniff glue. Now he soaked in the tub with baking soda trying to draw out the smell. And all so cheap cabinets made of simulated wood and particleboard could be put in double-wides. This was the life.

As they slid out of the booth to go back to work, Cole shot a parting glance at the girl who seemed to look down the years. Jimmy was too busy defending mullet cuts to notice.

—

Denise was at his apartment, having made careful arrangements for one of their sporadic encounters. Her husband, Zac, the road warrior, had gone to San Antonio, and she had left their little girl with Zac's mother, who was probably playing Noah's Ark or some other Bible-based game with her. Zac's family was like that. Not snake handlers, but Bible-as-life-manual folks. Zac didn't want his wife to have a job, and he even seemed displeased when she proposed to take some college courses. He suggested craft classes instead. Maybe he was afraid she would pick up some ideas and infect their airtight Christian home.

Cole didn't mind the occasional nature of their relation; in fact, he preferred it that way. He had been with women whose love was like kudzu. Denise didn't cling. She turned to him for relief from a squeaky-clean showroom marriage. Leaving her husband was out of the question, and Cole assumed she knew he wasn't marriage material. Still, he suspected she imagined him better, kinder than he really was. Her expectations had probably been lowered enough that he could meet them in two-hour installments. The two of them weren't just braiding the sheets all that time either. Some talking and listening got done. In a way it was kind of pathetic how little she asked of him.

"Do you remember the cafeteria hamburgers? We used to complain about them, but sometimes I wish I could taste one again. Silly, huh?" They had gone to the same high school. She had graduated; he had dropped out his junior year.

"I remember the group you hung with didn't want much to do with my kind. All during tenth grade I hankered for Jean Radisson. Mean Jean."

They had covered this ground before, including the fact that they noticed but felt nothing special for one another back then. What they didn't admit was how much nostalgia held them together now.

"I carried the torch for Bobby Thorpe. Once he smiled at me. I floated that whole week."

Jock. Cole had disliked the whole tribe. When the football team got pounded in the playoffs by their arch-rivals, he and his buddies celebrated down at the levee.

"It's good to see your taste in men has improved."

Denise didn't respond, and he realized almost instantly he'd said the wrong thing. He hadn't meant her marriage with Zac, but her being with him in this bed was always a reflection on it.

"I'd better get going. I've got some baking to do for the Daughters of Light meeting. They like their cookies extra chunky."

Among her other good points, Denise refrained from dumping whatever guilt and sadness she felt on him. More than this, she took his mistakes and somehow turned them right. Another woman might have left him holding an invisible bill detailing his debts, but Denise just stole back to that other world that was her main life, and wasn't.

———

The hiring freeze at the cabinet factory had the effect of squeezing more work out of those still on the line. Management said it was either that or wage cuts. Arkansas being a right-to-work state (Cole called it right-to-screw-the-workers), everyone basically looked out for himself. The line bosses put on added pressure to speed up the process, guaranteeing that the cabinets would be more mediocre than ever.

Cole's boss reminded him of the vice-principal at his high school, the type with a corncob up his butt. He couldn't stand anyone taking a bathroom break, always suspecting it was just a cover for a sneaked smoke. But if he left the shop floor to check, he knew he would be aped and cussed on the line. It was a dilemma. Cole didn't see the problem, because he knew from experience that one could have a satisfying long pee and short smoke at the same time. But lately he was careful not to provoke the guy, seeing as how he placed his chips on getting laid off, not fired.

"Shields, I thought we agreed you weren't going to wear that shirt to work anymore."

Cole glanced at the offending garment with its picture of a dreadlocked Jamaican holding an enormous spliff. "Oh, forgot. I'll remember next time, Mr. Derwent."

"See that you do. We're a family-oriented business."

Cole savored the absurdity of this comment; he would add it to his collection of stupid Derwent sayings. For the rest of the afternoon he amused himself with riffs on it. He even imagined having Mistah Spliff put on stickers, and placing them furtively on each cabinet as it came down the line. Every household could use a little reggae.

—

A few weeks later while his truck was being serviced, Cole noticed a book in the waiting room. Books had never seemed a good use of time, but the picture on the cover caught his eye. It showed a couple kids sitting in a goat-drawn cart waving small American flags. He could tell they were waving them because their hands and the flags were blurred. The book was a collection of photos from the town's early days. There was a TV in the room, but some woman had it set to a talk show, so he picked up the book and started to flip through it.

The pictures were arranged by decade, starting with the town's founding in the 1870s. Like a lot of other towns, it owed its beginnings to the railroad, which still ran through its center, hauling freight and snarling traffic. The depot had been torn down in the 1960s, after the last passenger train had come through. Cole's father still fumed about that, calling it one of the more boneheaded things the town leaders had done. There were several shots of it, inside and out, and Cole had to admit it could qualify as a landmark, something you might want to keep even after it had done its work. Like the downtown *Rialto*, which had gone the way of the bulldozer too.

All kinds of businesses had been photographed, some simple and bare, others well-stocked and showy. In the meat market a row of carcasses on hooks hung to one side, and behind a small display case with a register on it stood a chopping block. That was it. The general store, on the other hand, was crammed with jars, bins, barrels, bolts of cloth, and household devices. It struck Cole that while flour and pickles hadn't changed, the latest contraptions of those days seemed downright ancient now. Then again, other new and improved things were basic enough to last. One picture showed a muddy main street being dug up so concrete sewers could replace wooden ones before it was all paved over. Solid businessmen stood along the boardwalk surveying the project.

Cole laughed when he saw a shop advertising FURNITURE. UNDERTAKING. WALLPAPER. Maybe that was the kind of thing his company needed to do to stay afloat: cabinets for all occasions. The layoffs had begun, a development that didn't surprise, though the timing concerned him. He had a truck to feed, and unemployment to collect.

———

The following Wednesday, just as the shifts were changing, Derwent pulled him aside.

"Sorry, Shields, but we're letting you go. Business is slack. Stop by the office and pick up your pay."

Keeping low and holding his breath hadn't worked. The ax fell anyway. Just seven more days and he would be eligible for comp. He didn't want to mention this, so he tried a prefab story about needing to keep his job a week or so longer to settle a gambling debt with some guys who played rough. He figured that would fly better than some bull about an engagement ring or operation.

Derwent just repeated himself and walked off.

Cole felt like taking his glue gun and going taxidermy on him.

—

Through the weekend he treated his anger with beer and dope. Jimmy, Ty, and Lester dropped by to show solidarity and partake with him, but he knew they were relieved to still have their jobs. While he couldn't blame them, he also couldn't shake the feeling he'd been cheated, singled out for screwing. Between them they decided that the company timed it to keep him from collecting unemployment. Their plans for revenge grew so elaborate and wild that they ended up braying like jackasses.

On Monday Cole picked up all the bottles, emptied the ashtrays, and faced facts. He could pay his bills through the following month, then he'd be broke. His folks would help if he asked, but he didn't want to. So he would have a break from work after all, only shorter than he'd hoped, and on his own dime.

He didn't do much that week, apart from renting movies and listening to a stack of CDs he'd bought and never unwrapped. Denise slipped in and sympathized when she heard the news. She seemed more concerned about his situation than he was, and suggested places where he might look for work. She knew he was too proud to take any money from her. Besides, her husband kept a tight grip on the checkbook, and would notice any unusual cashflow. As she was leaving, it came to Cole that they both had problems now that the other really couldn't help, except to offer a little comfort.

There was another woman giving support too, even more shadowy than Denise. On and off he had been thinking about that girl in the photo at the barbecue joint. At first she helped him pass time on the line. She soon separated herself from the other women in his daydreams, though, because he came to have no part in this one. It was all about her. That made it tough; he didn't have enough words or pictures to bring her to life. Then he came across that book in the waiting room, and it gave him a place for her, a town with backyard sawmills and creamery wagons and lone college buildings. He also tried to recall the stories his Nana had told him that he never bothered to keep straight as a kid. She had known everyone, all the old families, their doings and misdoings. With nothing but time on his hands now, Cole worked up a likely story for this girl, something worthy of those clear eyes and free looks.

Iris. That was her name. It had taken him a while to discover because it wasn't like naming a baby in advance. He was coming at it from the opposite direction. Anyway, he decided that after graduating, Iris had kept living with her parents, an only child, and pretty much indulged. They knew they had a rare one that would only bloom on her own terms. So they got used to the parade of disappointed suitors and didn't push her to become a shopgirl or an elementary teacher. Instead, she took odd jobs, bottling Fizzoo Cola or serving as a dance partner at the Esquire Hotel socials.

It was two weeks now that Cole was unemployed, and he hadn't made any serious attempt to find work. That month's rent he'd covered, and he could make one more payment on his truck, but nothing more. His only income was some money he'd won at cards. He thought about going to West Memphis and having the greyhounds run it up. That would take some drive though, which he seemed to be lacking. Most days he sat around the apartment doing nothing much. At times he felt he couldn't face the world outside, with its wage-slave jobs and cattle-chute pressures.

Iris had made her own way. When the first radio station appeared in town, a thirty-watt affair housed in a converted toolshed, she wheedled a spot on the air. Maybe she started out reading from the Farmer's Almanac or passing along her mother's canning tips. Before long, though, she was playing gramophone records and making her voice familiar. It didn't pay, but she loved doing this new, fresh thing that seemed to come along with her in mind.

Like the biplane that landed beyond the cotton gins one day, a toy for a rich young guy who Iris knew fancied her. He probably jumped at the chance to take her up with him. They circled the town, and Iris was surprised how different it looked from up there, not like the map of it in her head. She enjoyed getting above it, the steady rush of air, the hint of danger. After the ride, she would have gotten him to show her how the controls work. In payment she would give him a kiss.

Cole was satisfied with her life so far. His own, however, needed some attention. Not wanting to flip burgers, change tires, shingle roofs, stock shelves, or mow lawns, he found his choices limited. There was an opening at a local amusement center, a place with a roller rink on one side and an eight-lane bowling alley on the other. The owner, an old guy, needed someone halftime to buff floors and generally help out. He could offer six an hour. Cole told him he would think about it, but he didn't intend to take it. The work seemed too custodial, a step in the wrong direction. Besides that, the pay and hours just wouldn't cut it.

After another week of dead ends, though, he began to reconsider. With part-time work he would be bringing in some money, and still have time to line up something better. Even then he would only be able to cover the rent, not his truck payments. And no way was he going to let it be repossessed. Biting the bullet, he sold it, paid off the loan, pocketed the difference, and borrowed a mothballed LeSabre from his father. He promised himself he'd replace the truck as soon as he got back on his feet. In the meantime, though, since the position was still open, he would be making ends meet at the roller alley.

To ease the bitterness he reminded himself that setbacks were natural, like the time his father injured himself and was off work for six months, or those floods that used to cover the town before the Corps got control of the river. He decided Iris, too, had had her losses, such as when she heard of a lynching one county over and couldn't keep a lid on her anger. She made a statement on color hatred over the air and got herself fired from the station. That adventure was over; now she would have to find something else.

—

Cole's new job wasn't so bad. Old Mr. Schnitzler really did need the help. The only reason he could keep the place going was that he owned it outright. Not many kids wanted to skate; most of the income came from the eight lanes. Sometimes Mr. Schnitzler would get flustered and hand out pairs of skates to bowlers. Certain kids tried to take advantage of him, claiming they had lost money in the vending machines or given him a ten rather than a five. Cole took to watching them from the counter and correcting their mistaken notions with a look they understood. He also did his share of buffing, retrieving balls stuck in the return chutes, machine stocking, and shoe maintenance. Mr. Schnitzler also turned over the sound system to him; Cole picked stations based on his assessment of the customer mix, a delicate procedure.

Even his first week Cole ended up putting in more than twenty hours. Before long he was over thirty. The cash flow at the place was improving, and Mr. Schnitzler could see it was due to his energetic new assistant, a young man with ideas. One day while rummaging in the storeroom, Cole came across some pinball machines buried under boxes. Digging them out, he realized they were classics from the '50s and '60s: Drag Racer, 7 Voyages of Sinbad, G-Man, and Space Station 2000. They all needed repair, and Mr. Schnitzler figured they wouldn't return enough to justify the expense. After some research, Cole suggested they sell one online and use the money to get the others running again. Mr. Schnitzler turned the whole thing over to him, and the next week a guy drove in from Michigan, thrilled to get a G-Man for two grand, even a broken one.

Cole had a simple explanation for the difference between this job and all his former ones: Mr. Schnitzler was the first boss he ever liked.

—

She was trying not to show it, but Cole could tell that something had Denise down. With things looking up a little for him, he felt he could shoulder some weight for her.

A few gentle, coaxing questions uncovered a couple connected problems. It seems the last time she was there, someone from her church saw her leaving his apartment complex. The guy mentioned it casually during fellowship, and she came up with an equally casual answer, but it had her worried. She knew the whole pack of them were trained sin-hounds. At the next Daughters of Light meeting she cracked. A friend of hers who had left the church recently miscarried, and one of the women used the word "visitation" to explain the loss. Denise flared, launching into this shocked saint. In the process she cast some fire and brimstone of her own on the church itself. Now Zac was very displeased with her, and insisting that she apologize in front of the whole congregation.

"I don't want to, but I may have to. I feel like they've got my scent now. Even coming here today I took a big chance. For all I know they've got a lookout posted across the street. With binoculars."

They both smiled weakly at the notion. Cole resented Denise's predicament, but he also disliked the sense of a net drifting his way. He had nothing to offer except temporary refuge, and even that might be blown. Only out of habit he kept up the lightness between them. "No more chunky cookies for them."

—

Why couldn't the main parts of life go right at the same time? This situation with Denise dragged at him, and he couldn't tell whether he was more upset for her sake or his. What did he expect, that a relation with a married woman wouldn't get complicated? And all because they happened to meet at a home improvement store. Well, that and everything that came after.

Rather than dwell on it, he turned to Iris. She had gotten through the Depression not noticing much difference. Life in Arkansas was always pretty close to the bone. Now that the country was at war, she saw her chance and took it, joining up to fly planes from the factories to air bases. After training in Alabama, she was stationed in California, whose big cities she came to love. She and her air corps friends would head to Los Angeles or San Diego on leave. There they would drink and dance with enlisted men, or with boys in oversized suits. Most of the time, though, she was shuttling planes across the country, feeling more free than ever. It was all movement and blueness.

Cole pictured her flying over Arkansas as he racked up the high score on the Space Station. With all three machines up and running, the quarters were starting to roll in. Mr. Schnitzler told him he had a head for business. As long as fun was the business, that seemed fair enough. He did have ideas for the rink side, which was lagging. If he got help from his buddies at the cabinet factory, he could build some portable ramps and attract the skateboarding crowd. Either that, or he could install props for laser tag. They could even use the scrub woods out back, which would make a good paintball site.

As they were discussing the possibilities, the phone rang. It was

Denise. She apologized for calling him at work, but she needed to talk. Zac had requested a detailed log from the phone company and confronted her about all the calls to his number. She claimed they were just calls to a friend, but Zac wouldn't buy that, and lectured her on trust and fidelity. Then he told her he was going to look into the matter further. She knew that wasn't an idle threat and felt she had to warn him.

Cole's head started to swim. He needed time to think, and he didn't want to air his problems in front of Mr. Schnitzler, so he told Denise to call him later at home. She shouldn't worry; he would come up with something.

———

He wanted to say she had to leave Zac and his lousy church. And go where? To him? He could hardly support himself, much less an instant family. Who was he kidding, anyway? Denise didn't need his advice; she only needed to trust herself. The more he thought about it, the more he expected a call from her gently but firmly breaking it off. Leave or stay, she couldn't afford him. He wondered whether he wouldn't mainly be relieved.

The end of the story: he had it now. Iris' last plane got past the inspectors with a fatal flaw in the wing. It came apart at ten thousand feet. A clear, bright day. It was perfect.

———

Denise hadn't called, and the next morning at work he felt weightless, suspended. As much as he wanted to put all the difficulty behind him, he knew that the loss of Denise would be a loss. It was like she had slipped into his life and been quietly strengthening the foundations all this while. In turn he couldn't quite say what he had done for her.

There was something else that needed righting. A pair of light grey eyes gazed frankly through his impatience and evasions. She hadn't simply flown off into the blue. She had returned from the war, come home, and eventually married. A lawyer from Little Rock. With pinkish politics. Over the next twenty years they moved together toward the front lines of the civil rights struggle. Along the way they lost friends and made new ones. He became a judge; she raised two children, and later in life had a career in public radio.

"Cole Shields."

He looked up from his buffing at a guy wearing a business suit and too much cologne.

"I'm Zac Prater, Denise's husband." He said it with authority, like a cop. Cole thought of the G-man he had sold. "I've come to tell you that your interference is over. Stay away from my wife."

Normally he would have flipped the guy off and walked away, but Cole stood his ground. "Is that what Denise wants?"

"Denise wants what I want, which is a marriage without falsehoods." The words sounded straight and pious, though Cole thought he detected some smoke.

"Why don't I just call and see what she has to say."

Zac hesitated. "No. She's at her parents' house and doesn't want to hear from you. We're working this out between us. You have no part in this. You've done enough damage." There was a thin hairline crack in his assurance.

"Maybe Denise is through with me." He paused, then added, "Maybe she's through with you too. The difference is, I won't pretend to think or speak for her. From what you've said, it appears she'll manage these things just fine on her own."

As he stood facing this righteous, blind, wounded man, Cole decided that there were gospel truths and gospel truths. He knew his own shortcomings. He believed that Denise saw other things as well. The way through this briar patch wasn't at all clear, but through it he would go. Through it they would see.

# THE IMPORTANCE OF SHOCK ART
Andrew Arslan
Volume I, Issue 4

Art can be almost anything: paint drips splattered across a canvas, a photograph of firefighters raising the American flag on 9/11, or even paintings inspired by pornography. As Andy Warhol once said, "Art is what you can get away with," and artists get away with plenty. There are works of art that are viewed as controversial, often earning it more attention. Controversies can create debates with a beautiful array of ideas and opinions exchanged among people as they justify their positions on a given work of art. Artists generally approach their art forms as a way to create meaning, or convey a message. At times these messages are misunderstood and never fully appreciated leading to a backlash and giving birth to the latest hot controversy in the art world.

"Shock Art" never fails at gaining attention and stirring up controversies. It tends to include images or acts in a work of art that would offend others, or at least definitely catch and hold one's attention to the work. One of the most well known works of shock art is *Piss Christ* by Andres Serrano. *Piss Christ* is a photograph of a crucifix submerged in the artist's own urine. The fact that the artist used his own urine may come off as disgusting to some, but that doesn't make the work any less artistic.

The photograph was taken in 1987, and has been the center of more than one controversy since then. In 1989, Serrano received $15,000 for his work, *Piss Christ*, which ignited a controversy from not only citizens that found the work offensive but also by United States senators. Senator D'Amato (R-New York), and Senator Helms (R-North Carolina) were outraged with the award given to Serrano because part of the $15,000 that Serrano received came from the National Endowments for the Arts, which is a publically funded institution. On the work, *Piss Christ*, Senator D'Amato was quoted saying in a letter to the National Endowment for the Arts Chairman Hugh Southern, "Shocking, abhorrent and completely undeserving of any recognition whatsoever. Millions of taxpayers are rightfully incensed that their hard-earned dollars were used to honor and support Serrano's work." D'Amato even went as far as ripping a copy of *Piss Christ* in the chambers of the United States Senate on May 18, 1989. Senator Helms told the United States Senate that, "Serrano is not an artist. He is a jerk." The events would lead the United States Senate to hold hearings on public funding of the arts throughout July 1989, in regards to the National Endowment for the Art's Appropriation Bill. An amendment in the bill that required the NEA to have 'general standards of decency and respect' passed both the Senate and the House of Representatives, and would later on be upheld by the United States Supreme Court in 1998.

Not everyone was actually opposed to the work, though. Art critic Lucy Lippard stated in "Andres Serrano: The Spirit and the Letter," *Art in America*, that *Piss Christ* "is darkly beautiful photographic image...the small wood and plastic crucifix becomes virtually monumental as it floats, photographically enlarged, in a deep rosy glow that is both ominous and glorious."

*Piss Christ* hasn't always been safely protected from people that have tried to attack the work when it has been on display. Just this year, on April 17th, *Piss Christ* was attacked in the southern French city of Avignon by a group of fundamentalists. The work was damaged by what is believed to be a screwdriver that slashed the photograph. The attack on April 17th wasn't the first attack on Serrano's *Piss Christ* either. Previously in 1997, in the National Gallery of Victoria in Melbourne, Australia, a man tried to remove the work from display. That incident was followed by an attack by two individuals, which led to staff members being injured. The two incidents led the gallery to shut down temporarily due to unsafe conditions created by the work's presence. Serrano's work has also been attacked in Sweden by a group of Neo-Nazis in 2007.

In the Lower East Side neighborhood in Manhattan, the Orchard Windows Gallery had been displaying the work of artist

Nick Weber between May 9th and May 27th. The *Porno Paintings* were inspired by stills from film pornography. His work, *Porno Paintings*, is a series of very explicit sex acts that have created a controversy in the neighborhood, and a backlash from parents, teachers, and by a church located near the gallery.

According to the *New York Post*, a teacher from a nearby school expressed his distaste for Weber's *Porno Paintings* at the Windows Gallery by saying, "That's pretty disgusting. Our kids walk by there. Our children shouldn't see something like that." In response to the criticism that Weber is facing for his paintings being displayed at the Windows Gallery, he has said, "They're afraid it's going to corrupt the kids, when kids can watch people getting shot on TV." The owner of Windows Gallery, Dino Eli was at first concerned about the work because it related to porn, but he felt as if the work was what the gallery was about, "an artist with a message."

The two artists have both been caught up in their own controversies, one on an international level, and the other at the local level, but the two ended up with similar reactions to their work. People have called for both of the artists' works to be removed from the galleries, and the interpretations of the two works were also very much misunderstood. Serrano's *Piss Christ* wasn't created in order to offend Christians, as many seem to believe. *Piss Christ* represents the misuse of religion to Serrano. In a report in the *Guardian* on the April 17th attack on *Piss Christ* in Avignon, France, Serrano had said that *Piss Christ* is a criticism of the "billion-dollar Christ-for-profit industry" and those "...who abuse the teachings of Christ for their own ignoble ends." Weber's work was also not made in order to offend others. He didn't want to use live models as some had suggested that he do because as he stated in an interview with Speliotis, "...it has to be from the Internet because that's what the world is now. You study an image of someone and paint them, you get to know them. It sort of rehumanizes [sic] the thing...it's not porn anymore."

There are also works of art that don't actually have a "shock" factor to them based on their subjects, but based on who the artist actually is. At the Sin City Gallery in the Arts Factory located in Las Vegas, Nevada, an exhibit titled, *Multiples,* displayed paintings by serial killer John Wayne Gacy between May 16th and May 25th this year.

The paintings were listed for sale at prices ranging from $2,000 to $15,000. The subjects that Gacy had painted involved clowns (he used to work as a clown), Jesus, Elvis, Hitler, Ed Gein, Al Capone, cherry blossoms and the Disney dwarfs. The controversy surrounding the exhibit wasn't solely based on the work being done by a serial killer but also by the proceeds being denied by the National Center for Victims of Crimes. Mary Rappaport, a spokeswoman for the National Center for Victims of Crimes stated, "Out of respect for the victims' families, we have not agreed and would not agree to accept any contribution that comes from the sale of John Wayne Gacy's work, which he did while in prison for torturing and murdering young boys and men," to explain why the proceeds would not be accepted by the organization.

According to the *Las Vegas Sun*, Wes Myles, the owner of the Arts Factory was quoted saying, "It's outsider art. It's primitive art. You can't be in a room with it without feeling. How can you say it's that weird when you've got shows like 'CSI,' 'Criminal Minds' and 'Dexter?' There's someone dying in every one of the episodes. Our society has a fascination with that," which draws a similar opinion on the matter as Nick Weber's statement on the reactions to his own work. Myles was also asked whether or not he expected protests, which he responded, "I hope so. To have intellectual conversation about art is positive."

The "Shock Art" movement has drawn both praise and criticism but it is constantly sparking conversations with each and every controversy that is created when each work of art is put on display. The movement has even inspired works of fiction, such as "NippleJesus," by Nick Hornby, which tells a remarkably similar story to what had happened to Serrano's *Piss Christ*, misconceptions were made on the artwork, *NippleJesus*, which led to its destruction. Just as in the story, and in reality, an interpretation held on a work may not always be true to the artist's actual intended meaning on a work of art. The "Shock Art" movement will continue to shock, and spark controversies, but ultimately it will create some of the greatest discussions on art and inspire others to create.

# GOOD HABITS
Jim Davis
Volume 2, Issue 2

I used to write with a different grip.
I tried it again today and slipped through time
to Ms. Porringer's classroom, where we learned
*Good Habits, Good Habits, Good Habits,*
and the importance of repetition, the retention
of specific brands of history, solid practice: she cut
glass in her free time, etching alpines in gravy bowls.
We spied on her, one recess, our soft sausage fingers
on the stone window ledge, our tousled hair and wild eyes
peering through the gap in the blinds. She tapped two
pens against the desk—eyes closed, singing soundlessly
to the radio, where Nina Simone crooned
*Oh but this whole country is full of lies*
*You're all gonna die and die like flies*
It's funny how memories can induce a freeze-frame
of consciousness. Today, with this grip, with Nina
singing in my mind, I can clearly see the image
induced by the lyric, a long strip of adhesive paper, peppered
with black flies, still buzzing. Two of the boys ran away.
But Billy and I stayed, staring at the raw nakedness
of her emotion. She stood to the chorus, *Mississippi Goddam!*
When we went back to class, we learned of oceans and continents,
colored an outline of Old Glory. For the rest of the day
Billy sat in the corner, staring. Jacqueline stole my pencil

but I didn't care. Billy went on to become an alcoholic, died in a boating accident. The warning signs were there: red sky when he woke, hung-over. Now and then, I pack myself peanut butter sandwiches and hold my pen incorrectly. Nostalgia, idealized: a memory of pain, or pain at memory. You never forget your first love, or outlive your curse.

# PATTY REVERE
Tim Sallinger
Volume I, Issue 2

## I

Patty empties her ashtray into the coffee pot to give it some flavor. One part coffee to one part sour Irish Creamer; Patty knows it's good till the last drop. She imagines herself in the Folgers commercial, as the sprightly ballet dancer who awakes looking radiant in a pink bathrobe to prepare her morning joe. Patty sports a moth-eaten baby blue nightshirt, draped across her large frame like a tarp over a swimming pool. After taking the first sip of her coffee, Patty sighs with relief like the dancer. Unlike the dancer she's barely able to get a breath out without four or five wet coughs. Hacking a wad of phlegm into the sink, Patty retires to the sofa in front of the TV to smoke three Newports before the last segment of "The View" has ended.

45-year-old Patty Revere doesn't leave her north side Pittsburgh one-bedroom very often. She never feels the need to. She's more comfortable watching the people on Full House or Family Matters. Nothing much seems to happen outside in those programs; if it does it's usually a special episode and seeing it disturbs Patty. When she was a child her father watched a show with her on the public access channel. Unlike her usual programs, it took place completely outdoors. The ground was made of dust and Jay told her it was the beach,

"Bleach?"

"No, Patty. *Beach.*"

and that you could walk on it for hours and not reach the end. Patty thought about all the debris that fell off her rugs when she shook them off, all the dust she'd swept out her back door. All of it had to go someplace. Maybe that's where beaches come from. All the dust bunnies and rug debris of the world combined to create a vast tan landscape, where people could walk all day.

A strange-looking red bug appeared, crawling on the dusty tundra. An invisible man called it a "hermit crab."

"Decapod crustaceans of the superfamily Paguroidea fashion their own habitats in a novel way.

'One beast's trash is another's treasure for the hermit crab: a discarded sea shell makes for a cozy home."

Patty awakes with a start when the cherry at the end of her cigarette falls on her thigh. She yelps and flicks it into the shag rug at her feet. The pain helps bring her out of the thick snooze brought on by too much spoiled milkfat. The doorbell rings and Patty realizes with a bolt of fear that it is the second time.

## II

Alex looks blankly at the peeling yellow paint on the door in front of him, and he thinks about what it would be like to run his finger down it.

When he was a boy he knocked on his neighbors' doors selling candies to raise funds for his school.

Somewhere in Africa a cheetah crouches unseen in a field of tall grass.

Alex scratches at a scab above his brow. Don't pick the scab.

If you pick the scab before it's healed you'll have a big nasty scar.

The cheetah smells the wind and scans the horizon.

Alex rings the doorbell again. Then he runs his finger in a long horizontal stroke across the width of the door. He looks at his hand and there are flecks of yellow. Rubbing his fingers together doesn't seem to help much. Transfixed, he picks at a hanging strip of paint. It peels off the wood like dead skin from a sun-burnt back.

## III

Patty doesn't understand. There is a cat at her door, scratching to be let in. It must smell the spilled creamer, or the empty cans of meat in the garbage. This has happened before, and Patty likes to let the cat in. She doesn't mind if it makes a mess out of her garbage or pukes the rotten meat on her sofa. But the cat has never rung her doorbell before.

Patty's vocal chords, unused to the exercise, slap together and issue a trembling call through the door.

"Who is it?"

"Alex."

Alex rubs his fingers frantically on his thigh. He looks down but the paint is still there. He hadn't thought this far ahead. What will he do if she doesn't open the door?

There is a long pause. Cars honk in the street behind him. He feels like he's standing on the bank of a river.

He hears Patty inhale through the door.

"I thought you were a cat."

Without thinking

"I am a cat!"

A pause. Patty inhales and clears her throat.

"May I come in?"

Both of them are surprised when Patty opens the door.

## IV

Patty has a clock. It stopped ticking at 3:27 p.m. years ago and she never took it off the wall. It still hangs over her kitchen sink and now she misses its steady rhythm for the way it seemed to fill the silence.

Silence is an uncomfortable rarity in Patty's life, but she felt she should turn the TV off when entertaining a guest. When there is silence just before Final Jeopardy, music starts playing to pass the time.

Alex looks across the small, sticky aluminum table at his hostess. Before him is a fruity-smelling bowl of creamer. His stomach growls and he thinks that perhaps he is hungry. Patty starts singing.

The cheetah, invited into the den of the antelope, is momentarily paralyzed with confusion.

Alex is tempted but wary. The singing only serves to put him more on edge.

Abruptly the singing stops.

"Are you hurt?" asks Patty.

The bowl of spoiled creamer is a pale pink hue. Another drop of red falls in as Alex looks down. The scab on his forehead is pinched between two fingers in his right hand. He hadn't noticed.

"Do you have medicine?" asks Alex.

**V**

Patty thinks first of Dr. Sanjay Gupta, but then she thinks of Rebecca, the woman who stops by to visit Patty every once in a while, and to bring her a plastic CVS bag. Inside the CVS bag are orange tubes with words written on the side, but Patty can't read, so she has to remember exactly what Rebecca tells her.

"This is medicine for you Patty. It make you feel better so remember to take them, okay? Is okay? You take your medicine Patty?" Rebecca would say.

Rebecca is very funny. The way she talks is funny, like the people on Channel 4 but slower and using words Patty can understand. The way she is so small but moves so fast around Patty's apartment, nimbly stepping over mounds of dirty laundry and VHS tapes, is funny. Patty can never do anything but nod when Rebecca talks to her because if she opens her mouth she knows she'll laugh and she doesn't want to hurt Rebecca's feelings. In the winter Rebecca wears a lime green coat and this is Patty's favorite, because with it on she looks just like one of those tiny green bugs, the kind you forget about until one day you look at a rock very closely and you see one scurrying across the surface.

"You can have some of my medicine. Rebecca tells me I have to take it to feel better, but she's just a silly little bug."

Laboriously, wheezing, Patty rises from her seat. The CVS bag is stashed under the bathroom sink, along with many others full of orange tubes from other visits.

"Rebecca's just a silly little bug. You can have all my medicine. I don't need any."

Alex claws through the bags, their contents spilling out at Patty's feet like the entrails of a fresh kill. Patty begins to laugh.

Alex looks up momentarily, the expired Prolixin capsules he was studying momentarily forgotten. Patty's laugh is harsh and raspy and doesn't decrescendo the way most people's laughs do, but instead repeats itself in a loop, like a broken laugh track. He pops a handful of multicolored pills into his mouth like they were Skittles. He starts to laugh too.

## VI

The Magic Bullet sits in the middle of a long marble counter top. Myriad glass bowls, each filled with a measured amount of ingredient, form constellations around it.

Patty and Alex sit at rapt attention as one by one eggs, sugar and cream cheese are poured into the device and subsequently pulverized. An ecstatic young woman in a salmon-colored cardigan pours the homogenized substance into a pie plate, a wan moon set among the stars.

Patty leans forward to flick an inch of ash off her cigarette onto the carpet and it vanishes immediately, whisked away to an invisible realm of forgotten detritus; kept company by gum wrappers and lint. Alex is cleaning himself in the manner of a cat, pharmacopoeia vibrating through his veins like a subway train on a loose track.

The camera cuts to an old woman. Upon seeing a cheesecake made in just five minutes, she raises her eyebrows disapprovingly.

Patty hears it first. "Ooh, another cat come to visit?"

Alex hears the second knock. "Pittsburgh police! Open up!"

Deer may freeze in headlights but not cheetahs. Alex is halfway to the back door when Patty starts to unlock the front.

## VII

A tall man with a shiny belt is driving a car. The car is painted in special colors and gives him special powers. The radio is playing. It's a commercial for a hardware store.

"Young's Hardware, where you can find just what you'd expect to find at a hardware store."

The tall man's fingers drum on the steering wheel. Signaling, he turns left and squints into the sun.

He likes this commercial. He also likes the hardware store. He's met the owner of the hardware store, and he likes him.

The tall man drives his special car through the town all day, and he looks at the houses and the people who live in them and he thinks, "This is alright."

The tall man is very dangerous.

A crackling noise announces the arrival of a coded message on his radio. He interprets the message and presses a button on the center console. Incredible lights and a very loud noise erupt from the special car as it accelerates through traffic.

Moments later, the shiny car rolls into an empty space in front of Patty Revere's squat aluminum-sided house. The sunlight reflects off its hood fiercely, making it glow like a tanning bed.

The tall man approaches the yellow door. He knocks.

Then again.

"Pittsburgh police! Open up!"

The paint on the door is fading. The tall man waits.

The noise of latches coming undone is the same noise vermin make when they've infiltrated the walls of a house, scurrying and scratching. The door opens and reveals Patty looming tall in her blue nightshirt.

"Ma'am we've had calls about a man trying to force entry into your neighbors' house. White, five foot nine, blond hair. A cut on his forehead."

He ended the sentence by bending the pitch of his voice upward, as if he were asking a question. But it wasn't a question. Patty was confused.

"Nothing to worry about, we're acquainted with the perp, just a local pill-popper. Someone thought they saw him on your front doorstep."

Patty continues to stare implacably at the tall man. His words are complete nonsense to her. But she lets him prattle on because she's struck by the way his clothes are so clean and crisp. His belt is very shiny in the noontime sun.

A cheetah is pressed against the aluminum siding of Patty's home. His heart pounds blood through his head like someone was boxing his ears. He is staring at the special car.

Alex sees himself in the car, feels his foot against the gas pedal. He imagines drumming his fingers on the steering wheel and squinting into the sun. His vehicle rolling down wide suburban thoroughfares and potholed city streets. Through the window he sees the citizens of Pittsburgh wave at him and smile. They wave out of respect and smile because they admire him.

Alex waves back and as he does he can feel the starched epaulet of his shirt rub against his shoulder. Looking down he sees he is wearing the uniform of the tall man, shiny belt and all.

He presses a button on the center console and the car becomes a howling banshee, flashing its multicolored lights like a toy. Other cars submissively drop out of view as he accelerates onward, faster, faster, exploding fuel in his heart and a stampede in his gas tank.

## VIII

Alex barely makes it to the door handle. The tall man is on him with the righteous zeal of someone whose privileges are endangered.

Patty screams for no reason she can articulate.

A cheetah and a man do battle before her. The man is armed with technology but the cheetah is wild: scratching, biting, hissing.

The man prevails. Patty remains at her door, wailing like a kettle.

Alex spits and cries from the chemicals in his eyes. The tall man rises to his feet, his quarry subdued and restrained. He lingers there, his legs astride the beast.

"Ma'am, I'm going to ask you to calm down. Please calm down ma'am."

Patty will not calm down. She watches the tall man standing over her cat, sees the scratches on his arms and face from the recent struggle. Alex is lying on his side sobbing, pulling his knees towards his chin with his hands still cuffed behind his back.

Patty can not hear the tall man because she is no longer standing on her front porch. She is standing in the woods with her father. At her father's feet is a bleeding doe, in his hands a rifle. The doe lies on its back in a perfectly inert state, its haunches splayed open frankly, the tendons in its legs having lost their ability to constrict.

Alex is lifted rudely to his feet. Blinded, he's led to the special car. The tall man pushes his head down.

With a large knife Jay begins to slash the doe near its hind legs. Sticking his fingers into the gashes he tugs and like an onion the beast loses its skin. Underneath it is red and purple. Patty screams and she will not calm down. Dead leaves crumble under her boots as she turns and runs. Jay calls after her and she hears him but she will not respond.

The tall man is about to turn to tell Patty that if she doesn't calm down, he'll have to put her in his car too. He doesn't get the chance. The impact in his lower back makes his arms flail out at his sides and his knees buckle. As he falls his forehead slams into the car in the same spot where Alex's would have if he hadn't pushed it down.

Alex makes a yipping noise more reminiscent of a hyena than a cat. Blinking, he rolls out of the special car and joins the rag doll on the ground. Patty has stopped screaming, her massive chest heaving. She is slowly coming out of the woods.

After frantically fidgeting with the keys attached to the tall man's shiny belt, Alex rises to his feet, his hands unbound. He runs to the front of the car and jumps in, gesturing wildly to his friend Patty, who, after hesitating for only a moment, steps over the tall man and into the passenger's seat.

The inside of the car is clean and smells like nothing. Alex smiles at Patty and brings the car humming to life. He leans over to press a button in the center console. Patty gasps and then giggles as the car lights up and plays a song. Alex drums his fingers on the steering wheel and squints into the sun.

# GRANDPA REVISIONISM
## John Grey
Volume 2, Issue 3

Grandpa had a hundred fingers on his right hand.
Grandma counts them in her sleep.
He was almighty, all powerful.
Being with him was like
being a sea wall battered by storm and tide.
And yet his voice...she says
it was an orchestra:
tender violin, strident brass,
the clash of cymbals,
the hard and angry drummer man.

He went to war.
She's surprised they needed anyone else.
And he built the house
she's lived in all these years.
Axe-man, Paul Bunyanesque
and he kept the fireplace burning.
They had no radio
so he sang to her,
made her laugh.
For the longest time,
no electricity.
But he shone more light
than anyone.
he was ten thousand candles,
none dripping.

He was a million lamps,
glowing from his eyes.

My mother says when he was alive
they argued, battled, day and night.
But love's not love
until it's risen from the dead a little.

# THE SEXY DANCE
Oline Eaton
Volume I, Issue 2

It is hard to know how to be a girl. Because there is this notion that there are good girls and things that good girls mustn't do. Things that get good girls in trouble. Like, say, dancing for instance.

I made my dance debut at the age of five. Midway into the can-can in a recital so long that my parents only ever refer to it as "that nightmare where our butts went numb," my pink sequined strap broke. Through the remainder of the show, a significant portion of my left nipple was visible, indiscreetly bobbing up over my costume's blue satin and yellow fringe.

This is a perfect snapshot of my relationship with the art of dance. It always pans out sexier and more scandalous than I intend.

I didn't dance with anyone, much less a boy, until a blind date in 1996, when my best friend set me up with her church crush to determine whether she liked him more than her date. As happens in all perfect plans, we rendezvoused at McDonald's.

In the photograph that my best friend's mother insisted on taking, we stand against a brick wall like delinquents in a line-up. The glow of the golden arches refracts off the oil on my face and my brown leather bomber jacket, brown velour dress and brown patent shoes. My mouth is curled into the smirk of a democrat who knows she is on a date with a teenaged republican and about to ride in a car festooned with a sticker in support of Bob Dole.

As the shutter clicked, she said, *Perfect, ladies.*

At homecoming, we engaged in that self-conscious style of dance particular to school-sponsored events set in cafeterias. The kind where you remain always at stretched-out arm's length for fear that groins or chests will touch. Chaste moves undermined by the fact that we were executing them to Boyz II Men's "I'll Make Love to You."

As the Boyz implored us to throw our clothes on the floor, I swore I would never do this again. It was too embarrassing. Too fraught with the potential for the awkwardness of bad breath and colliding loins.

I didn't dance again until the summer of 1998 when, during a Cornell University-sponsored dance, a boy, who may or may not have been wearing glasses, asked if I wanted to dance with him.

That night, my dorm-mates and I had frolicked about our floor like loons, playing Madonna at such a volume that the hall minder warned us that ladies shouldn't be so loud. That was why, when this boy asked me to dance, I said yes. Because before we had even gotten there, we had decided we were not ladies.

I know we danced to Destiny's Child, but I don't remember much about this boy himself beyond the fact that he struck me as unconscionably bold for someone who looked like Doogie Howser. He had asked me to dance though he did not know my name. His right elbow had grazed the edge of my left breast as we walked onto the floor. And at one point while we were dancing, his hand slid across the dip of my belly above my jeans, though the immediacy with which my entire body tensed ensured his boldness ended there.

I don't remember this boy because even though we danced the rest of the night together, I never once faced him. Instead, I faced outward, with an expression that suggested I was merely scanning the crowd with cool nonchalance while someone engaged me in dancing of which I was unaware.

What I remember is hands and arms and elbows. The feel of denim on denim. Gratitude that I wasn't wearing a dress. And that this was not what I had thought dancing would be like.

This pre-dated my exposure to hip-hop videography, so I did not yet have the vocabulary to identify what we were doing as "grinding." This, I see now, was a small mercy, because grinding was a terribly awkward thing for a seventeen year old Southern Baptist girl to be doing with a boy she did not know.

At the time, I was embarrassed, but not by what we were doing. That was beside the point. Rather, I was embarrassed by being in such close proximity to an actual living, breathing boy. Of him being that close to me, privy to pieces of myself I could not see. The curve of my neck, the curve of my ass, the back of my hair. And yet, I felt safe because he was a stranger. The terror would have been unimaginable had he been someone I knew.

There are no words for how naive I was then. How incredibly uncomfortable I was with the area I inhabited, the space I took up. I did not know what to do with my body.

I never ever ever ever knew what to do with my arms.

After dancing with denim boy, I still didn't but, if anything, I had a newly inflated false faith in my own abilities. I had danced. Therefore, I thought I now knew how.

So that October, when another boy asked me to homecoming, I leaned over the square of desks in the right front corner of Mrs. McAbee's homeroom and solemnly told him to "be prepared." I fancied that this sounded sexy. It probably made it seem to him that dancing with me would be an ordeal requiring many hours of practice and prayer.

As in all rites of passage, we were kids playing adults. And, as nearly always happens at such times, our failure was spectacular.

He wore a butter cream button-up through which his Hollywood 27 Theater grand opening commemorative t-shirt could be clearly seen. I wore a red silk dress my mother had made that inexplicably ballooned out between the shoulder blades, as if in anticipation of the sudden need to accommodate a backpack inside.

In the photographs of this moment- which my parents ran to the Kroger 1-Hour Photo that very night to have all produced as 8x10s- we look sanguine and just the slightest bit shell-shocked.

This was my first real date. Ever.

We dined at Waffle House. Because I had walked away from a *Cosmo* article with the firm belief that lettuce was the food men most liked to watch women eat, I ordered a salad.

And then, at the dance itself, I busted out my moves.

I stood dancing before this dear boy. In the lenses of his glasses, I could see the lights bouncing off all my shiny surfaces. Bewitched by my twinkling allure, his eyebrows shot up. Overwhelmed by my refined beauty, he took a step back. Then, intoxicated by my charms, he looked deep into my eyes and he said, "Caroline, your hips are being too provocative."

It is hard to know how to be a girl. To cross your legs at the ankles and keep always your knees closed. Your body says too much. It gives you away, before you are ready. There my hips were being all provocative and I barely even had a grasp on what that word meant. We'd only just learned it in Advanced Placement English the week before.

I was suddenly aware that I had done something wrong, though I did not know what. I had only been dancing. The only way I knew how.

It was a matter made all the more perplexing when, the following Tuesday, this boy passed me a note written in purple ink putting forth the assertion that we needed to date. Immediately. Exclusively. Because I was perfect.

It is hard to be a girl because it takes a really, really long time to get over the notion that there is a certain way we girls must be. This idea that we must always be good. That there are things that make us bad. That there are things good girls do not do and that if you do them, you will not be loved.

I envy my younger self in the pictures from that first recital. My nipple bobbing indiscreetly above my costume's blue satin and yellow fringe. I remember no embarrassment in that moment. I remember dancing and that is all.

We danced together again. At prom later that year, that boy and I. Three weeks before, we had sat together under the air vent in Barnes & Noble. On the worst hair day of my life we had held hands as he told me he was gay and I had laughed because that seemed the only thing to do.

At prom, his shoes were too slick. They made a crunching noise when he stepped. My stiletto had gotten stuck in a street grate and my dress hem had torn. We performed "the Tennessee Waltz" on a dance floor that was entirely too small so that, doing our box steps, we circulated like horses on a carousel mistakenly shifted into high gear.

We were not perfect. We never have been. We needn't ever be.

We dance, though we do not know what to do with our arms.

# THIS IS HOW A HEART BREAKS:
## The Myth of the Dying Reader
### Sarah Martinez
#### Volume I, Issue 3

*A writer is first of all a reader—a reader gone berserk, a rogue reader, an impertinent reader who claims to be able to do it better.*
—Susan Sontag

There's a chair, brown comfy leather that they sit in at the coffee shop where I write. Today it's a teenage boy, yesterday it was a girl. He was reading CS Lewis, I don't know what she was reading but I do know it as a library book. I get the same feeling when I see this as I do when I see people holding hands or kissing on the street: hopeful and optimistic about the future. We're not as angry and hopeless and screwed up as some would have us think.

My favorite author, Junot Diaz, said in a talk once that he felt happy every time he saw someone with a book in their hand. I know the feeling. I think: *Ah, yes, one of my tribe.* My people. They get it— they get me. So imagine my disappointment when I read what he had to say about the future of writing and literature in an interview he did with Dave Eggers that appeared in issue # 33 of McSweeney's. He expressed concern that the academic world is not producing as many readers as writers. How is this possible? On the other hand, maybe this is a much-needed observation, I wouldn't know, thankfully I don't exist in that world. In my world all sorts of people are reading.

I heard once about another writing teacher who had to bribe his students to read and subscribe to literary journals. These were MFA students mind you, not high school students. These same people were going to be writing and submitting to literary magazines, and expecting to be published, people I imagine bemoan the fact that book sales are down and lit journals are closing their doors. This guy had to actually bribe his students with extra credit to get them to subscribe to these same journals they would be submitting to. Junot Diaz's comments speak directly to this problem of declining readership in the academic world and I go: *Yes!* Like Jamie Lee Curtis in *A Fish Called Wanda,* I writhe on the floor moaning, "Speak It. Speak It!"

So why, after I got done nodding my head in agreement was I worried? I love him. I mean: I Love Junot Diaz. It got so bad, and I talked about him so much, that at one point my husband started having bad dreams about this guy. Not only is he a brilliant, earth shattering literary force, but he is also a teacher in the best sense of the word. You can hear it in his voice when he speaks and writes about everything relevant to an emerging writer: MFA programs, reading, art—on that subject he has tons to say—and even global activism. His political comments make a frightening amount of sense. He also blurbs for certain genre novels and even admits to watching and enjoying TV. In short he is a remarkable human being, and I am grateful for him and totally bummed that I couldn't agree with my whole heart as I usually do.

The line that ended the interview, the knife through this reader's heart was this: "I just hope we've created enough readers that when the book club meets up it's not just me and you."

These words left me feeling afraid and lonely. I tried to explain my frustration to my husband and at the same time try to figure it out myself. Hubby responded with a blank look and a generous smile. After an hour on the elliptical, several emails to friends and the beginnings of two blog posts, what I finally came to is this: I can't believe Junot Diaz—my hero—has been corrupted. How could he ever doubt? Maybe the academic setting is something else—probably it is. But on this side of the planet people are still reading; all sorts of people, old people, children, stressed mothers and I know this is hard for some to wrap their heads around: teenagers.

This obviously is not a scientific study, everything I offer here is anecdotal, but hasn't anyone else gotten frustrated with this sort of talk? Please tell me I am I not the only one. I felt that for once someone should offer something positive instead of the same old doom and gloom about how no one is reading, publishing is falling apart and if you're a writer you better just not bother trying to publish unless you have at least 1,000 fans on your Facebook page. I will refrain from dropping the sorely needed F bomb.

I was a reader since before I could even read. I played with the books my parents had in the house and then as soon as I was able to process the words I started in on *Jaws* and even got two pages into *Anna Karenina* before giving up on the pretty blue hard cover. I stuck with *Jaws* for a few weeks, finally giving up somewhere around page seventy—I was in the third grade. I was in the fifth grade when I finished *Jaws* and read *Sybil*. Again I'll say it, I was a freak.

My YA was CS Lewis, Peter Benchley, Clive Barker, Stephen King and Edgar Allan Poe. I believe in the evolution of the reader. I started on this stuff: the fun, bizarre, scary and weird. With this I built the concentration and muscle to be able to get in to other things I was curious about or learned about from other sources. A Metallica video led me to *Johnny Got His Gun*. That led me to war stories and historical fiction. Would I have started with these? No.

An editor suggested recently that I read Balzac's *Lost Illusions*, which was written between 1837 and 1843, where the anxieties about publishing seem strikingly similar to the way people talk today. And then there's Henry Miller's *Tropic of Cancer*, written over seventy years ago. Same old, same old. It seems writer's anxieties haven't changed much in two hundred years. We're always convinced we're brilliant and at the same time convinced no one wants us.

In 1996 Jonathan Franzen, (who published two hugely successful literary novels after this interview, and after the technology boom) David Foster Wallace, and Mark Leyner appeared on *Charlie Rose* discussing the notion that people were not reading "Important Books" anymore. Tell that to my boyfriend at the time. He hadn't read anything more challenging than *Hustler*, chided me every time I picked up a book, and called me "a reader," like it was a disease. One night I read to him from Hemingway's *Old Man and the Sea*, and boom, he was off. He had gone on a fishing expedition a few years before and he connected at a very deep level with the story of an old fisherman and a big fish. He loved that book and read it cover to cover. After that you know what he did? He spent a month reading *Moby Dick*, every night. He was so excited. He told me all about Ishmael like he was a real person. I actually thought he had lost his mind—I never saw the need to pick that one up myself.

When I read to him one of the short stories of Anton Chekhov he sat still for it and even expressed outrage at the female character's behavior toward the young prince we were reading about. He may not have been a voracious reader but writers long dead spoke to him on a very deep level indeed. This is important. The experience was big for him, someone who never got through high school, someone who never thought they would ever like to read, and he did it for pleasure.

I don't know if he ever picked up a book after that. But I will always remember the way those books changed him, turned him on in a new way even for just a little while. If even a dedicated philistine (who had access to music, TV and movies) chose to spend his time pouring over a dead man's words, I know books and their ideas are not going away any time soon. Reading is an experience essential to being human, even if every single person on the planet doesn't get it, even if only a fraction of us do. The need to connect at a deep level with another mind is something that will never go away, no matter what other distractions are available to us.

My friend's daughter is tearing through all of the *Junie B. Jones* books and gives me huge smiles when she talks about them. She is in the second grade. My goddaughter read the entire *Lemony Snickett* series when she was eight, and then started *Oliver Twist* after I broke one of my own rules and gave her a big fat Dickens anthology for Christmas (I threw in several smaller books as well.) What about all the toddlers I see at story time at the library, all the kids who attended Samantha Vamos's book signing last month? Their parents push reading like mine did, probably more.

YA and children's literature are big markets, if you doubt this just look at the agent and editor lists for any upcoming writer's conference, not to mention the statistics available from the Association of American Publishers. If TV and iPods and computers were going to replace the experience of reading it would have happened a long time ago.

When did the TV come out? How long have we had PC's? What about movies? My goddaughter was born after all of these and still she chooses to spend her time reading. Is that because our schools are doing such a great job or because she found out early how totally cool it is to get lost in a book for ten hours, and that nothing else can do that for her? She also has a Wii, a TV, regularly goes to the movies, and owns a Nintendo DS. Amazing. Does this do anything to renew our faith in books? I find it comforting in a time when even our most respected authors seem to doubt the power of the very thing they've chosen to spend years of their lives working on.

I love movies. When you add a beautiful or quirky actor, or actress, scenery to die for and a powerful soundtrack they can take my breath away. TV occasionally has something to offer as well—don't get me started on *Dexter*. The experience is still limited—it exists only in my eyes and ears—it has to filter through these to get to my mind. The images and sensory detail in a book go straight in, there is no filter. Movies and TV will never replace books. Ever.

When Marco Vassi in *The Other Hand Clapping* writes, "Through the open window, nature throbbed," I can imagine that if someone tried to show this in a movie it would look something like one of those atmospheric deals where the green of the trees outside is electric, florescent, and there could be that weird humming in the background like you had in those movies from the 1970's. But when I read this line in a book the words move straight through my consciousness and can do so much more. They can crack me up, or call on my associations of nature and things that throb. My mind makes up its own images, at a much faster rate than a television of film image ever could. If I am in the mood to be generous, I might even stop and contemplate his choice of words and what else he might be trying to say so I can get even more out of reading the sentence.

The kids around me look to be shaping in to hardcore readers just like me. My toddler picks up a book, even if the TV is on, carries it around the house, running her fingers under the words and speaking something that sounds like the rhythms of the real words. Often she brings the book to me and demands that I read to her. My six-year-old has no problem with most of the words in front of her and will read to me, her father, or her little sister if asked. Her favorite books are based on the characters in *Scooby Doo*. Take from this what you will.

My goddaughter's parents did not graduate high school, nor do they read much, if at all. Still somehow they spawned someone who can't get enough of this dusty old habit of reading. My husband can still count on one hand the number of books he's read in his life, so from three people who don't read, three people who do will take their place. The future looks bright indeed.

I am not bringing up these kids to say I have much responsibility for their readership. I hardly see my goddaughter. I spend more time with my writing than reading to my kids, and still…still, they are picking up books. If these kids follow the same pattern I did, first reading purely for escape and entertainment, it is likely they will at some point turn towards something more, to learn, to be expanded, to have fun, and if they find the right writers, these can happen all at the same time.

I believe in the experience as it happened to me. I developed the habit young, and my tastes changed. In the beginning I was not reading "Important Books" but reading for pure seat-of-my-pants fun with *Jaws*, then after a while I wanted to go farther, get to know my characters a bit more and to satisfy my curiosity about what after all was the big deal, so I read *Lonesome Dove* and *The Satanic Verses*. In my later twenties I found Richard Russo and I was off on a whole new adventure. Had you given me *Empire Falls* when I was thirteen I would likely have set it aside for something with some monsters and serial killers.

I can still hear my mother's words, "Garbage in, garbage out," all through high school, then in my twenties when I came home with *Great Expectations*, "*Who* is reading literature?" The funny thing there was that I never saw her read anything that wasn't related to politics or world events. For me there was a process and an order to the way I came to know great books and I am still grateful that I can go back to *Carrie* and *The Dead Zone* when things get hard, it's my comfort food.

I study Jonathan Franzen's work and listen to him talk about writing for advice and insight in to the process. He writes so smoothly and with such honesty that I feel I am communing with a family member every time I read one of his essays even if I don't always agree with him. He is so intent on blocking as much of the noise of our modern society that he works on a computer that doesn't get Internet, and he wears earplugs to block out the noise of the world around him. Every time I get sidetracked in the middle of a good work session by my email program telling me I have an email from someone I had been waiting to hear from, or worse blow a half hour on the Internet because I just had to jump on and look up one tiny thing, I remember everything he said on the subject of interruption. And like the irascible child with a patient parent, I roll my eyes and make a face. He is right, right, right.

Still, something about the larger implications of Franzen's example worries me. I don't like thinking I should feel guilty for indulging in the more insipid parts of our popular culture. It makes me feel like there is something wrong with me. Why can't I read *Freedom* in the afternoon, with the twitter and Facebook enabled phone inches away, watch *Dexter* at night, read *Tropic of Cancer* on my kindle—shooting quotes from that wonderful book all over cyberspace, encouraging other people to read it in the process—and listen to P!nk or Marilyn Manson on my run, or while I write? Why does it feel like it has to be one or the other?

I get the sense that the crux of the fear is that all the other types of entertainment could possibly replace books. Can you believe it? Oh big literary writers of little faith. Like no one else but you ever fell completely in love with the experience of reading. Maybe me and my friends and relatives are just anomalies. Ok, fine, maybe when we die the whole experience will die with us. Oh, but I forgot, there are all these young people I mentioned before...

As a reader when I hear our most widely revered writers going on about how TV and iPods and computers are going to steal readership I get crazy, I want to scream and I feel betrayed. If these writers themselves don't believe in the power of books when those of us— simple readers, not recipients of any big awards or acclaim—have faith and continue to love, collect, and read, how can they doubt?

Nothing for me will ever replace the power of the written word, whether it's on a Kindle, a piece of paper, or a computer screen. Ever. The words will enter my mind, and wrap themselves in all the stuff that's already in there: memories, words from previous authors, random associations with TV, music, advertising, and all the facts I learned in school, and make something universal yet distinctly my own experience. Nothing else can do that. Nothing at all.

I love books. I believe in books. This dirty habit is mine and I'm not giving it up, and I don't believe it will be that easy for anyone else to give up either, not once they've been hooked like I was.

# DOUBLE EXPOSURE
Adrian R. Magnuson
Volume I, Issue 3

I remember her body,
a child's body,
small breasts
under a dirty white shirt
tucked into black silk pants
her sleeves rolled up
exposing skinny arms
with knobbed elbows
first akimbo
then, as I continue to remember
raised.

And her face,
how it was tilted up,
how the light struck
leaving shadows
from her small flat nose
from the tight curl of her lower lip
from her protruding chin.

And her hair, dark, black,
no—blacker than that,
how it ran down
over one shoulder
some stray strands
crossing the bridge of her nose
in thin black lines
others caught between her lips
pursed.

I imagine her body,
older,
flattened
under a black silk ao dai.
unadorned
her sleeves rolled down
concealing skinny arms
with knobbed elbows
she lets hang at her hips
then, as I continue to imagine
she raises.

And her face,
how she tilts it down,
to let the light strike
painting shadow
from her forehead
sweeping dark across her features
now curiously missing.

And her hair, dark, gray streaked,
no—grayer than that,
how she bunches it in a knot
at the back of her neck
some stray strands
crossing the bridge of her nose
in thin gray lines,
others she parts to reveal her lips
open but silent.

And her skin, tan and creamy,
No—lighter than that,
and that brown smear
slanting across her cheek,
where she had rubbed
the back of her hand,
now drying to dust but still
wet and streaked.

And her neck,
not large enough for her head,
and longer than it should have been,
draped loose in beaded chain
my two steel dog tags dangling
free in the soft vee
of warmth and flesh
above her open collar.

And her stance,
standing barefoot in the mud,
feet apart
one pointed forward
one planted back
spine arched—shoulders angled,
one lifted forward,
one dropped back,
stiff and motionless.

And her hands,
the left held toward me
as if in greeting,
but in the right, a rock
raised up behind her
a muddy rivulet
running down her arm.

And her skin, nut brown.
No—darker than that.
She tightens the furrowed lines
slanting across her cheeks
curving around her eyes
her ears, her mouth
and dust clings
in the deep creases.

And her neck,
not large enough for her head,
stretched like a chicken's,
and wound tight in beaded chain.
She presses my dog tags
deep in the sunken vee
of sinew and artery
above her buttoned collar.

And her stance,
standing barefoot in the mud.
She holds her feet together
both pointing outward
flat and rooted
back drooping—shoulders uneven
one up a little
one down a little.
She is limp and quivering.

And her hands,
the left reaches toward me
as if in desire,
the right clutches the polished tags
in a gnarled grip,
and I see the tarnished chain
running down her arm.

And her eyes,
hooded in epicanthic fold,
black and level
watch me, or not
look at nothing
look inward
look past
into the past
into the distance.
A hundred yards?
A hundred miles?
A hundred years?
Away.

# BALANCE, GRACE, AND HUMILITY
Sonia Lyris
Volume I, Issue I

I came to Argentine tango with all the humility of a martial artist who's been practicing fighting arts for three decades and all the grace of a woman who thinks formal dance is a waste of time.

Grace? I throw people across a mat, do wrist locks, take flying falls. Fight with Japanese sword and sticks. I got your grace right here.

Humility? Absolutely. Japanese martial arts are all about humility. We have heaps of humility. We keep it in the fridge so it's fresh when we need it.

As for Balance, I can do those karate kicks, the ones where you stand on one leg and knock someone over with the other one. That should do it for balance.

Or so I thought. Turns out that spinning musically on the ball of one foot while wearing heels and making it look easy is a slightly different thing. But I didn't know that yet.

Grace, humility and balance. Before tango, I figured I had them all in sufficient amounts.

## DOING IT IN HEELS
I dance three, four, maybe five times a week, hours at a time, often without stopping. Mostly in heels.

Way back, long before tango, I used to say that heels were a tool of patriarchal oppression and bad for your feet besides. Some years later I ventured into the alien land of wearing one-inch heels and thought myself brave.

When I started tango, I wore flats. Months went by and it became clear that I had to at least try the heels. Intellectually I was sure it wasn't possible, but my eyes showed me that I was wrong, that indeed some women could dance this hardest of all social dances in heels many inches high. There they were, actually doing it.

So it had to be possible. Insanely hard, perhaps, but possible. There was something about the challenge that got my attention.

## TANGO AS LOVER

One day after I've been dancing a couple of years it hits me that tango is like a temperamental Latin lover, a guy who can make me feel like the best kiss ever one night and cheap candy the next. I find that while he isn't often gentle, when he's sweet it's the kind of night that you want to write about and get published.

Personalizing tango helped me deal. It focused me on my relationship to the dance rather than my interactions with the other people on the floor. It's not about them, I realized. It's not that I'll never be good enough, and not about comparing myself to other dancers. It's about my relationship with this thing, this dance thing. This metaphorical guy.

Tango and me, going out a few times a week. Dating. Seeing how it goes. Enjoying the magic when it's there. Bitching about each other when it's not. Fighting. Making up.

And, sometimes, crying.

## ANOTHER ROUGH NIGHT

It's another rough night. On the floor I feel clumsy and my shoes don't feel right. All my favorite partners are dancing with other people, not even looking at me. I sit at a table and fidget, trying to pretend I'm fine.

I remind myself that there are going to be bad nights. You can't take them too seriously.

Well, you can.

I'd been dancing about eight months. I was sitting outside the dance on a warm summer's night, trying not to cry. One of my teachers came over, sat next to me, and asked me how I was. Haltingly I explained that nothing I could do was right, every move was a mistake, and that I wasn't sure I was any good at this. He laughed, truly amused, and told me it wasn't as bad as I thought.

I was somewhat affronted at this lack of respect for my pain. Tango was serious business, worthy of effort, worthy of tears.

But he was right and the memory of his laughter that night has seen me through more rough tango moments than he knows.

Tonight tango-as-lover is being rude again. Crass and thoughtless. A real jerk. I try to let it roll off my back like water off a duck, but instead it stings my eyes and leaves a bitter rejection-flavored taste in my mouth. I stuff my shoes in my bag and leave.

Maybe tomorrow night will better.

## HUMILITY
You can't dance tango without being watched, and watched by some people who are much better at tango than you are. Once you realize that, you start wondering just how you look. Maybe you're really good. Or horrid. You invent stories. They are watching you. They're not. They think you've doing great. They think you're a terrible. The stories only stop when they stop.

I'm out on the floor dancing and I wonder who's watching, what flaws or elegances they can see in me. I'll steal a moment from my dance to glance around to see who might be looking and of course at that moment they're not looking at me.

If they ever were. Maybe they don't care enough to watch me at all. Somehow that's worse.

Humility is not about telling yourself that you're not that good. It's about knowing people might be watching you, judging you, and being okay with that, because their judgment is about them, not about you. It's knowing that truly, all the way down into your stomach, your legs, and most especially into your feet.

I have moments like that. Sometimes whole nights. They're magical, sweet, liberating, heady. A step from bliss.

### A DAY AT THE RACES
I don't know if I do this for fun, but I do it often.

I'm at a milonga, a formal dance, stripping off my motorcycle gear and tossing it under a chair to reveal a cute, tight black outfit.

Contradictions are a big part of tango. The martial arts background. The girl who thought dance was a waste of time. The heels.

I dig through my shoe bag and discover that I've left the shoes I meant to bring at home. Instead I have the 4 inch heels. Blue with leopard spots. Not subtle.

What the hell. In for a penny.

It's a formal dance, so there's even more people watching, sitting around, socializing. It is said that in the milonga, everyone sees everything.

Do I care? Tonight, it seems, I do. I feel clumsy, but not as clumsy as other nights. There's a touch of grace that I can almost catch.

And there it is: insecurity and confidence, judgment and surrender. It's all part of this game, hearing the voices in my head, watching the stories go by, staying with the music and my partner and all the other dancers. While making it look easy.

## BALANCE

Balance turns out to be a much harder challenge than I thought it would be. Months after I start tango it comes clear to me just how bad my balance is and has always been.

To do this dance I'm forced to admit to myself that I'm a bit afraid to walk on fallen logs and curbs. I start pushing myself. Telephone poles, curbs, balance beams, rocks, anything I can find. I'm facing the small fears in the hopes of understanding the bigger ones.

Just walking onto the dance floor takes courage, conviction, and a certain amount of denial. Egolessness, if you can find it.

Balance in tango, like everything else in tango, is both physical and personal. You have to stand on your own while staying in close contact with your partner. You have to take every motion thrown at you in the dance while somehow making each move seem like it was your idea.

You have to let someone else spin you like a top while gracefully getting the musical thing right, then seamlessly stepping somewhere else and doing it all again.

And don't forget to make it look easy. Like it was no big deal. Like you do this for fun.

## THE BEST COMPLIMENT

I'm at a practica, an informal dance, and I see Ted, an advanced dancer I met early on who I haven't danced with in at least a year. Ted is a very fine dancer, a lead who has studied for over a decade. He's very, very good.

When I started tango I'd stumble over my own feet trying to guess at what he wanted, hoping to impress him, determined to prove myself worthy of the time he took to dance with me. Psyching myself out.

To my surprise I'm no longer intimidated by him but my appreciation for his abilities has expanded as my skill has matured. His interpretation of this particular music, music that neither of us has heard before, is so good that I'm both stunned and delighted at his lead. I laugh aloud. He grins back. We dance and it's so much fun I remember why I do this insanely hard dance. Now, right now, it's so worth it.

We dance an hour and then more. I have to leave but I don't want to. I tell him I have to go and he begs me to stay, just one more dance. After that he pleads for another.

As I reluctantly tear myself away, hugging him one last time, I realize that I've just been given the best compliment of my tango life.

## HIDDEN IN PLAIN SIGHT
There's an unspoken fetish among tangueros for the secrets of the dance. We consider our advantages in the dance. Me with my decades of martial arts Another woman with her decades of dance. A cutie with her, well, her cutie-ness. We wonder if it's enough. It's not.

We lust for the secrets of tango that we don't have yet.

Year after year I learn more about what I'm doing on the dance floor in three inch heels and tight dresses. About the stories in my head, my insecurities. About the pride and the anguish of putting myself out there night after night.

Year after year I look for the answers to my movement challenges, how to do a particular move or how to smooth things out.

And year after year I find those answers, or at least the next layer. The advice of my early teachers comes back to me over and over and, stunned, I realize that I had the answers from the start. I didn't understand them as I understand them now, but there they were. I wonder how I'll understand them tomorrow.

As is so often the case in life, the answers were right in front of me.

It's not finding the answers that's all that hard. It's understanding the questions.

Maybe the mystery of tango is that it is, in itself, the question.

## GRACE
I learn this stuff slowly, at least by my own measure. In the last few months, finally, I've had some dances where I felt like I really knew what I was doing. I probably don't, but who cares? For at least for a few moments, sometimes whole songs, I could make my body do graceful things while keeping the partnership alive.

Clumsy words. Let me try again:

It's like making love in moonlight on a warm summer's night that somehow has no mosquitoes, on ancient, soft moss, with the warm scent of flowers drifting across my delighted skin. With a lover who knows me, flaws and all, and adores me all the same.

On the dance floor, whoever I'm dancing with is standing in for this imaginary lover, this archetype who is tango-as-lover. But the dance, no matter how intimate and amazing, is not about him. Even though tango is so much about the embrace, this hug in motion, connection and intimacy, in a very real sense, I'm dancing alone. The intimacy is there, but it's an almost universal intimacy. It's dancing with the archetype.

When it comes to real grace, we all dance alone.

## AMNESIA
I went to my first lesson to prove to someone that I really truly loved them. So much that I'd try tango.

Once. I expected to try it and be done with it, and I already knew what I would say. "Dance just isn't for me. Sorry, darling. It was fun. Charming. Really."

But it wasn't. Instead it was like the best sparring I'd ever done, the kind where you key in on the other fellow, and you're so well connected, seeing each move so intensely that it's like you're reading each other's minds.

Except it's to music and you're not trying to hit each other.

It was magic, that first time, but an hour afterwards I couldn't remember it. I went back the next week, and the magic was there again, but an hour later-- amnesia. So I went back again. And so on.

The thing that kept me coming back was so foreign to me—dance? Dance?—that I couldn't seem to keep the memory alive after. But I kept going back.

That seems to be the hallmark of good tango dancers: a stubborn persistence that borders on the insanely obsessive.

## SECRETS OF TANGO
Sure, in tango women do lead and men do follow. But by and large the men lead and the women follow. It's a sexist dance. Go argue with the Argentinians.

On the plus side, when you do take the other gender's role, serious tango dancers take you seriously, and they expect you to bring it. Don't just do the moves, but embody the archetype. Bring it.

So I do. I take the man's role and lead. I try to explain to new leads what it means, how to embody the archetype, how to bring it.

I've learned that the attitude, the archetype, the spirit I bring to the dance is as important as the moves. When I bring it through my body, it helps create the grace and balance I crave. It's not enough, but it's essential.

When I'm on the floor teaching, I tell my secrets freely. I share what I've figured out. So often my golden insights, my gems, just lie there on the table between us like seeming fakes, like platitudes, like trivial basics.

I struggle to explain that the greatest secret is that the seeming basics aren't, that they are the heart of every fancy move. But most beginners don't want that. They want what's next. It's hard to convey that the next step is the one we're doing. They don't get it, any more than I did when my teachers said the same things years ago.

The secrets aren't hidden.

## MAGIC
I watch a stranger on the floor. He looks like he knows his stuff. As the evening goes late and the crowd thins, I make eye contact with him, give him the capeseo. He nods and we step onto the dance floor together.

From the first moment I know I'm in for something different. Time adjusts herself subtly to accommodate a sudden, powerful connection and the seconds drip by like fine viscus honey. Each movement he makes evokes in me the best dancing I've ever done. One song ends and we move into the next as if we've rehearsed it a thousand times, as if the gods are smiling down upon us. As if we're in love.

This is tango gold. Maybe diamonds. Sparkling, solid, the real thing. This is the dance so many of my dances long to be. Before I know it, we've danced a glorious half hour together. It's beyond amazing, it's an experience I've only dreamed of.

He's from out of town, here on a rare trip. Chances are good I'll never see him again, let alone dance with him. But that's okay. I've come to accept these moments as they are.

To have drunk deeply of such magic means not expecting it to be other than it is. Like love. Like life.

## TANGO IS THERAPY

One of my teachers says tango is therapy. We all bring our issues onto the floor. Tango asks you to look at all your insecurities and fears. It pushes you to see where your cracks are.

It offers 10 minute love affairs that rival the real thing, and bring up all the same feelings and patterns.

I say that tango is a mirror. It shows you who you are and where you are. Whether and how you look into that reflection is a big part of the deep aspects of this dance.

It's such a hard dance, and I'm really not a dancer. Or am I? A strange thing, to consider myself graceful enough to call myself a dancer.

In a way, though, the dance is not really about the dance. I don't do tango to get better at tango. I do tango to get better at me.

# DIVINE LAPSES OF SENSE
Marc Polonsky
Volume 2, Issue 2

I took an interest in poetry because I had to. In 1990, as a community college English composition teacher, I was assigned to teach a course on American poets.

"I'm petrified," I told a friend, an accomplished poet and fellow teacher. "I probably know less than my students do about poetry."

"That's not true," she assured me. "You know plenty. You know what images are. You know what rhythms and metaphors and symbols are. You understand the difference between connotation and denotation."

"Sure, but that's just the basic stuff."

"Maybe, maybe not. But just start from what you know and go from there. You'll be fine."

So I did (and was). For ten years I modeled for my students a kind of Zen beginner's mind approach to reading poetry. Not: "The poem means whatever I think it does, because that's my experience of it." But rather: "This is what I see, so let's begin with that, and then see if we can take it any deeper."

Of course, there was often a fine line to weave between treating a poem as an expedition into the wild and viewing it as a Rorschach blot. I wanted my students to learn patience (just as I was learning it) with what could be observed about a poem, while not falling into careless solipsism. But if they did occasionally get all self-referential on me, I generally accepted this as preferable to Fear of Scholarly Error. A favorite cousin of mine once remarked (at a time when I was experiencing chronic insomnia) that sleep is a little like sex: once it becomes a ground of struggle, you're simply in trouble. I think the same can be said of poetry appreciation.

My favorite poet at the time (and, actually, probably my favorite still) was Emily Dickinson. I loved how her liberal employment of abstract nouns with capital letters led so naturally to discussions about connotative meanings, while a tight narrative logic nonetheless tunneled through her poems like a train—with only occasional (and highly provocative) lapses in what I like to call *sense*.

One poem I used to go over with my classes was Dickinson's poem #501:

> This World is not Conclusion.
> A Species stands beyond—
> Invisible, as Music—
> But positive, as Sound—
> It beckons, and it baffles—
> Philosophy—don't know—
> And through a Riddle, at the last—
> Sagacity, must go—
> To guess it, puzzles scholars—
> To gain it, Men have borne
> Contempt of Generations
> And Crucifixion, shown—
> Faith slips—and laughs, and rallies—
> Blushes, if any see—
> Plucks at a twig of Evidence—
> And asks a Vane, the way—
> Much Gesture, from the Pulpit—
> Strong Hallelujahs roll—
> Narcotics cannot still the Tooth
> That nibbles at the soul—

It is astonishing to step back and note how few concrete nouns Dickinson uses here, how heavily weighted this poem is to abstraction: World, Conclusion, Species, Music, Sound, Philosophy, Riddle…

Arguably, "World" and "Music" are nominally concrete, because we hear music and perceive the world through our senses. Yet these terms are so general that they may also qualify as abstract.

Creative writing teachers normally stress the importance of *concreteness* and *specificity* to convey a *tactile* experience to the reader. But Dickinson never took a creative writing class, nor did she ever try to publish her poetry, so I guess she didn't care. Yet no one (I don't think!) would contend that (for example) Poem #501 lacks visceral power.

One word that my students and I always had fun with here was "Species." What on earth could Dickinson have meant by *that*? A species of *animal* that exists beyond this world? Probably not. A species of *experience*? Maybe. Some students opined that "Species" was a semantic stand-in for "God." Fair enough!

My task (as I saw it), in "teaching" this poem, was to walk students through it, line by line, phrase by phrase, trying to ensure that everyone was at least *considering* each nuance with wide-awake eyes. We generally came to some consensus regarding what Dickinson was talking about, which was something like this:

*There is something beyond the world we know, which attracts ("beckons") us, yet remains a mystery that has puzzled the wisest people alive since time immemorial. No matter how brilliant a person is, in the end, at the moment of death, he or she must pass "through a riddle"—that is, into what is unknown and unknowable. Seeking to attain insight into the nature of existence beyond the grave, "men" have paid a tremendous price, enduring scorn and persecution. Yet people will grasp at any scrap of a clue (any "twig of Evidence" or "Vane"), often conceiving a fragile yet resilient spiritual faith.*

Strangely, it was usually towards the end of the poem, just as Dickinson generously slips in a couple of concrete nouns—"Pulpit" and "Tooth"—that divergent interpretations tended to cluster. "Pulpit" was no problem; we would rapidly agree that a Pulpit must be a Pulpit, as in a church. But "Tooth"—arguably the strongest punch-packing word in the whole poem—*that* concrete noun had to be a metaphor—but a metaphor for *what*? Conjoined as it was to the abstraction *soul*, Dickinson's selection of the word "Tooth" gave us a lot to chew on (sorry).

(Incidentally, believing that there are no coincidences in life or in Dickinson's punctuation, I often pointed out that she had chosen *not* to capitalize "soul." *Why not?* I would ask, if there was time for that discussion too.)

To my mind, the "Tooth" is fear of death, plain and simple. But I seldom said as much, because my students had more interesting ideas: Yearning for God, yearning for perfection, religious doubt, moral guilt…perhaps "Tooth" could mean all of these. Why not?

But regardless of the meanings and connotations of the Tooth that nibbles at the soul, Poem #501 contains no logical lapses, no moments where an attentive, analytical reader can only scratch her head and say, "*Huh?*" Poem #501, colorful language and copious abstractions and ambiguities notwithstanding, is a consummately rational little poem.

By contrast, the other day I was looking at Dickinson's Poem #600:

> It troubled me as once I was—
> For I was once a Child—
> Concluding how an Atom—fell—
> And yet the Heavens—held—
>
> The Heavens weighed the most—by far—
> Yet Blue—and solid—stood—
> Without a Bolt—that I could prove—
> Would Giants—understand?
>
> Life set me larger—problems—
> Some I shall keep—to solve
> Till Algebra is easier—
> Or simpler proved—above—
>
> Then—too—be comprehended—
> What sorer—puzzled me—
> Why Heaven did not break away—
> And tumble—Blue—on me—

Now, I think I pretty much "get it" up until the last line of the second stanza. Dickinson is saying that when she was a child, it puzzled her that the force of gravity caused even the smallest objects ("an Atom") to fall towards the ground, and yet the sky, or "the Heavens," which she assumed must be very heavy, "stood" above without falling, and without any "Bolt" (ha ha!) that she could see to fasten it upward.

But who are these "Giants" she's talking about? Her parents? Adults in general? Probably one or the other, I suppose.

The third stanza, however, is where sense, for me, disintegrates. Life has presented her with problems so difficult to solve that...*what*?

> Till Algebra is easier—
> Or simpler proved—above—

I feel sure "Algebra" must be a metaphor, but for *what*? Things proven in dependable, formulaic fashion? Things that make mathematical sense? Is Dickinson suggesting that our earthly challenges are so complex, they make the heavens appear simple by comparison?

My gut tells me that this "explanation" is too simplistic. Algebra "simpler proved"—an equation more easily completed—in the heavens: What type of equation could this be? And am I even asking the right question?

> Life set me larger—problems—
> Some I shall keep—to solve
> Till Algebra is easier—
> Or simpler proved—above—

Look at the *temporal* relationship here. She is going to keep larger problems to solve *until* Algebra is easier above. Why is she "keeping" problems to solve? Is she doing this on purpose? Or is this just a roundabout way of saying that her problems will not leave her *until...*?

Is she suggesting that her problems will not be solvable until the mysteries of the heavens are clarified as well? Is there some sort of Judgment Day concept at work here?

Again, I feel in my gut that this conjecture is too simple. Or, in any event, incomplete.

The more I chase the meaning of this stanza, the more it leads me in circles—or maybe ellipses or ovals. Interpreting these lines is, for me, an insolvable equation. So finally my mind relaxes a little. I have to fall back on feeling instead of analysis.

I feel relief at the idea of "Algebra easier or more simply proved above"—that seems enormous, even though (incidentally) I never had much trouble with algebra. Now, if Dickinson had used the word *trigonometry* instead, that would be a different story. Ha ha. Of course, then again, *trigonometry* is a clunkier, far less poetic word than *algebra*. Woolgathering even further, consider literal differences between the two. Trigonometry is concerned with spatial relationships; algebra with relationships between undefined variables. Hm. Undefined variables…Dickinson is particularly deft at generating electricity between those. As is God.

The fourth stanza resumes the logic of linear time. "Then"—that is to say, *after* whatever the third stanza signifies has transpired—that other mystery that had "sorer puzzled" the writer can also "be comprehended": only "Then" (presumably) she will understand why Heaven did not "break away" from the sky and fall "Blue" on top of her head.

If I were "teaching" this poem in a classroom, I imagine we would have a discussion on the connotations of the capitalized word "Blue," which Dickinson uses twice in the poem. "Blue" may have countless associative meanings. (I'm sure, for example, that there is a suggestion of "Heaven" in "Blue", as Dickinson drew much of her inspiration from church hymns. Many if not most of her poems can fit snugly to the tune "Amazing Grace," including the two poems presented in this essay, as well as darker pieces such as "I Heard A Fly Buzz When I Died.")

But again, what exactly *happened* in that third stanza?

For me, in that gracious moment when painstaking analysis cannot quite suffice, when my mind's capacity to fit the poem's words into a coherent (if somewhat far-out) conceptual schema has to break down, the poem comes alive, and offers itself whole and irreducible to my imagination, as something wiser than my mind.

This does not happen with every poem of course, nor does my "not understanding" a poem necessarily make it profound or effective. But I have learned to trust the seamless integrity of Emily Dickinson. I have never left a Dickinson poem with a sense of having been flimflammed. I find many of her poems to be like medicine, overthrowing the tyranny of my arrogant intellect when I allow them to gently do their work.

I believe we all need a break from our arrogant intellects, whether or not we deem ourselves "intellectual." Another way to say this is that we need respites from our egos, that part of us that is so *convinced* by our own stories about what makes sense, what things mean, what is reality, and where we stand in it. We need to "let in some air" so we don't stay too firmly glued to our accustomed paradigms. Poetry, at its best, accomplishes this for us.

So lapses of sense are not always nonsense. Nonsense is undisciplined and random. Lapses of sense, when they occur in the poems of visionaries like Dickinson, are breakthroughs into areas of thought and perception that cannot be codified into conventional language.

In a prosaic sense, all I'm really talking about here is *perspective*. Good poetry offers not just a fresh perspective on life, but a fresh *way of thinking*.

For me, this may be poetry's most powerful gift. It often (surprisingly!) feels like precisely what I need when other resources in my life fail to address needs that I cannot even name.

# Apiary

Catherine Warren
Volume 2, Issue I

This yellow swarm intends me harm
I watch its raid with no alarm
No thought of aid as cavalcades
crawl on my skin; a buzzing shade

a purple din. They enter in
my nose, and load my eyelids closed
with pollen dust. Antennae thrust
as compound eyes survey their prize.

In dreamy trance thoraxes trace
direction dance. The apis race
has found in me a princely hoard,
a treasury. My hair transformed

to honey stores; my marrowbone
foundationstone. My gate agape
lets drones escape, to mate in air,
die, solitaire. What once were pores

now buttressed cells immortal be;
As hive-mind roars, my body spells—
eternity—

# THE MOUNTAIN'S SHOULDERING WHITENESS
Gareth Spark
Volume I, Issue 4

Sarah Monaghan settled on the balcony of her new apartment, above the Casa Domenech. The night had settled deeply above Cambrils and she looked across the busy square: past the circling scooters and the diners waiting in line outside El Posit; beyond the small Moroccan girl collecting litter in the dusty darkness, to the sea—a silver moonlit glimmer between the high buildings with oval windows, the white masts of yachts like a dead forest, on into nothingness.

She sat high on one of the two plastic garden chairs the property owner had left for them on the tiny stone-paved balcony, drumming her fingers on the painted blue iron. When she and Tommy first looked around the apartment, hours before, she'd been afraid, physically, to step out and look down from the eminence of three floors onto the Placa Posit. She had countered the fear as Tommy slept in the one hot bedroom: first, she flicked through the TV channels, lost amid the blaze of Spanish and Catalan; then she had inspected the tiny kitchen and, finally, the shower, the drain of which, she was dismayed to discover, was crammed with broken pieces of concrete and other construction detritus. She had paused to examine her travel weary face in the bathroom window: her tangled red hair tumbled across pale shoulders, and her eyes shone, glinting flames in the mirror facing. She could barely see into the glass and stood on the tips of her short feet—once, twice, three times, her eyes appearing and disappearing as she struggled. She was tired; it had been a long trip, driving with Tommy across the country to Blackpool, where they visited her mother, and then down through the dark to Liverpool, where they sat on the cool grass, watching the first light of the world break dimly through the blue clouds of the east.

She smoked endless Lambert and Butler cigarettes, seated there in the dust and gravel, her back pushed against the broad glass panes of the airport lounge, watching Tommy pace, the air filled with dew and the chill of dawn. He noticed her attention: 'What?'

'Nothing.'

'You're regretting it now, aren't you? I can tell.' It was more of a statement than a question, and he dragged deeply on his cigarette, the glow of it illuminating his thin, hawkish face.

'No,' she smiled. 'Not at all.'

'It's the chance of a lifetime.' He laughed and sat beside her. 'I know that the last couple of weeks have been a bit, you know, harsh, but you've got to think about it the way I do; think of the stress we've had to put up with moving; all the planning, the selling of things; getting rid of the flat.'

She looked at him and smiled as she had learned to do. The breeze was warm as bathwater and there was an ache to it, infused with the perfumes of the rousing earth and that cigarette he'd flicked away and which lay between them and the fields ahead, smouldering like a star at the foot of the dawn. She knew what he was referring to: he'd spent the last few weeks working in his mother's pub in the Yorkshire moors, though it was obvious to everybody that his mind was already settled in the south and that wrapped up in his mother's apron strings was the last place he wanted to be. He'd fought with his mother, who resented, as always, the boy's heart being with his father, and Tommy had in turn vented his spleen on Sarah, who had always been there, who was a little afraid and desperate to cling to him because she did not believe there was anything else, anywhere, for her.

She'd woken a few hours later, when the Easy Jet plane was high above the Pyrenees. Her head rested on his bony shoulder and she looked up, through the dirty oval window at a deeper sky than she had ever seen. His clothes stank of old sweat and smoke and she pushed herself up from him. The lights in the aircraft throbbed and hummed, a dull amber that seemed to catch all this moment of escape in a timeless bite; the teeth of some kind of dream, touching and slicing between her old world and something new and unsupported. She felt bodiless for a moment, part of the sky and it was simple to ignore the machine then, easy, with her river green gaze fixed on that sky staring back at her. She sat up in the tight, uncomfortable chair, catching her knees on the plastic desk pulled down from the back of the chair in front and leaned over towards the window. Tommy's head fell to the other side. His mouth flopped open. She pushed closer to the light, lifted herself up, and glanced down, expecting nothing but cloud, the rolling, grizzled mat drawn over the last she had seen of England. There were mountains; white as fresh bone, stretched across the earth's shoulder as far as she could see; the peaks interspersed with deep ultramarine and green valleys, but always the pale blaze of the peaks, reaching up as though calling to her. She had never seen a mountain before, and to see these first, from the empty heart of the sky, touched her.

She shook Tommy's shoulder. He opened a sticky eye and turned to her: 'What?'

'Look out the window.'

He leaned over and glanced down. 'Oh yeah.'

'Don't you think it's beautiful?'

'Aw,' he said, 'not as beautiful as you.'

'I'm being serious,' she said, turning away.

'So am I,' he said, sounding exhausted, 'it's one of the many, many reasons I love you like I do.'

'I hope that's not just something to say.'

He smiled to himself when she'd said that, as though that statement spelled out her debt to him a little too blatantly: that she needed him, perhaps more than he needed her.

The plane shook and, suddenly nervous, Tommy said, 'I fancy a drink.'

'What a shock,' Sarah said.

'Is there a problem?'

'No.'

He frowned. 'I like those little bags they bring your whisky in, makes you feel like an astronaut. Wonder what the food's like?'

Sarah had shrugged her shoulders and turned back to the window.

She stared into the mirror in her apartment now and tried to recapture the feeling, but it had gone, too quickly. The place smells of that citrus tang the strong sun leaves on skin, she thought, holding a pale, thick forearm to her nose.

The living room was small and she sat down alone on a creaking sofa bed upholstered with dark orange cloth dotted with white designs. The television faced her, playing an American movie dubbed into Spanish: actors hurling words that had no natural nest between their teeth, arms flailing to the lisping rattle of Castilian churned through the speakers.

The patio was open, the door knocked gently in the breeze; she heard somebody laugh in the square below and she regretted ever leaving home.

# SUCH A GOOD MAN
Jason Fraticelli
Volume 2, Issue 3

Whatever it was, they had covered it with a thin blanket. My mother began crying and my father held her as we watched two men in blue uniforms carry the long cart out of the Bowlan's home and slide it into the ambulance. One of the men said something to Mrs. Bowlan and I saw her shake her head, then retreat inside and close the door. The man shrugged, walked back to the ambulance, and it went speeding off down the street. My mother, father, and I staring after it.

That afternoon my mother began cooking. She cooked for the rest of the day and then began again the following morning. The air was sticky with the earthy fragrance of dough rising and melting cheese. The cinnamon sweetness of an apple pie bubbling in the oven kept me panting at the door. My mother shook a wooden spoon at me and said "Quit hanging around this kitchen like some poor beggar child. This food is not for us. Now go outside for a little while."

Later that afternoon my mother called me back inside. My father sat on the couch in the pose he used for lecturing me about the ways of life: shoulders squared off, brow knitted firmly, hands clasped together in front of him. My mother crouched down and looked at me in a way that made me want to hug her and cry in shame for all the bad things I'd ever done.

"Remember Mr. Bowlan, lived next door to us?" The image of his bald, freckled head moving back and forth above the hedge as he mowed his lawn flashed through my mind. And how he would slap the newspaper and yell about rising taxes to my father as he left for work. "Well, he's passed away. Just yesterday. Remember the ambulance?" I nodded, my eyes shifting between the two of them.

"Would you help me carry some food over to Mrs. Bowlan?"

"Okay," I mumbled, my shoulders slumping with disappointment. Giving the food away was one thing, but being told that I had to help her do it seemed doubly cruel. My father patted my shoulder then went back into his study. I followed my mother into the kitchen.

She loaded up my small arms with the quiche and an apple pie, taking a casserole, a Jell-O mold and a bag of rolls herself. As we stood on the front stoop waiting for Mrs. Bowlan to answer the door, the warm apple pie I held tortured me with its sweet scents. I could only dream that Mrs. Bowlan would ask us to stay for a slice. Perhaps topped with a mound of vanilla ice cream that melted as soon as it touched the crust.

"Hello, Mary," my mother said as the door opened, sunlight illuminating the thin figure of Mrs. Bowlan. She shaded her eyes with a spotted bony hand, squinting as though she hadn't seen the sun in days.

"Elizabeth, how are you, dear?" she said, smiling a little.

"I'm so sorry about George," my mother replied shaking her head. "He was such a good man. We brought you some food so that you won't have to worry about a thing while all this is going on."

"Well, isn't that sweet of you," she said, directing her thanks to me rather than my mother. "Won't you both come in." I looked up at my mother to get confirmation from her that it was alright. She gave me a slight nod and I entered in front of her.

I'd never actually been inside their house before. The closest I'd come was the front porch where I often found myself shyly asking if I could retrieve a ball I'd knocked into their backyard. Mrs. Bowlan would always smile, pat me on the head and tell me that she would get it and not to worry. Then I could hear the muffled bark of Mr. Bowlan from the back of the house. She would return a moment later with my ball, a quiet look of fatigue hanging from her face. As she handed it to me she would always say "do try to be more careful dear," then shut the door.

Their house was very different from ours or any I could remember having been in before. Green and yellow striped wallpaper plastered their living room, making the white walls at our house seem bare and uninteresting. All of her furniture was made of dark woods with decorative carvings and curls that gave them an interesting look but not a comfortable one. Even the air gave off the impression that it had been floating around, unused for years. Their house reminded me of something I'd seen in an old movie, and I hovered close to my mother for fear of leaving the slightest fingerprint on anything. I followed Mrs. Bowlan and my mother to the kitchen, keeping my distance, unsure of what I was to do next.

"You can just set all those right on the counter here," she said indicating a spot next to a sleek looking silver toaster. "I thank the both of you so much. You can't imagine how much this helps." As quickly as we were able to lay the food out on the counter Mrs. Bowlan reached her shaky hands to snatch the dishes away and began meticulously arranging everything in the refrigerator, as if she had planned out where she would put it all before we even arrived.

"Well, it's the absolute least we can do Mary. And if there's anything else at all…"

"I said I'm fine dear, just fine," Mrs. Bowlan cut in sharply. After she had finished putting everything away she turned back to my mother with a smile and said "would you care for something cold to drink? It's awfully hot out there."

As Mrs. Bowlan and my mother talked, I wandered over to a screen door on the far side of the kitchen facing the back yard. I'd never seen back there other than through the slots between the boards that separated our yard from theirs. Everything looked like it had been laid out by an architect. A series of pots that lined the house rose from smallest to largest. All of the garden beds were perfectly squared off, an equal distance from the fence. It reminded me of something out of one of my math books.

What captured my attention most was a perfectly rectangular patch of dirt near the back corner of the yard. I could see a row of what looked like green feather dusters popping up out of the dark soil, and a row of thin green stems with red orbs causing the branches to bend under their weight.

"What's that?" I blurted, pointing out through the screen.

"Honey, it's not polite to interrupt while people are talking," my mother scolded me. "Mrs. Bowlan and I were in the middle of a conversation. Now, if you want to say something you'll have to wait your turn."

"Oh, don't be so hard on the boy," Mrs. Bowlan said walking over to me.

"What is it you got over there?" I pointed once again across the yard.

"My vegetable garden? That's where I get all my vegetables. As many as I can anyway, never did care for the store-bought."

"You make your own food?" I asked in astonishment.

"Haven't you ever planted a seed and watered it and cared for it until it grew up into something wonderful and delicious?" I shook my head. "My, my. What do kids these days do with themselves? You can just come right outside with me and I'll show you all kinds of things. You don't mind do you, Elizabeth?" she said to my mother as I followed her out into the yard.

"Are you sure it's not too much trouble, Mary? I know you must have a lot to do with the funeral arrangements and all."

"All that's been taken care of dear. Won't take but a minute."

"Oh, well, alright. You behave yourself, Miles," my mother said placing her hand just below her neck, the way she did when she was surprised or nervous.

In our yard the grass looked sad and wilted and grew in uneven patches. Their grass felt firm beneath my shoes, as though I were a giant, walking on thousands of tiny green pillars that crunched beneath my feet. There was so much color here, and all of my senses were drenched in a lively fragrance purer than anything I'd ever experienced before.

"Here, do you recognize these?" she said, pointing down to a row of leafy greens with reddish tips.

"Is it lettuce?" I asked recognizing them from the grocery store.

"Not just lettuce, but red leaf lettuce. Even better. And these here are my tomatoes," as she reached to caress one of the plump globes with her knotty fingers. "Do you like tomatoes?"

"Yes," I replied with an urge to grab one right off the vine.

"Well then, I have something for you. But we'll get it later. Look here." She crouched down to one knee and plucked something from a tangle of green vines. A strawberry, glowing red and beautiful. I could actually feel my eyes sparkle as she held it out to me. "Go on, eat it," she said, smiling a little at the delight on my face. I popped the whole thing in my mouth like a piece of popcorn. It burst between my teeth with juices slipping down my throat, so tart they made me pucker. "How do you like that?"

"We eat the ones from the store," I blurted.

"All the ones you see at the store were grown just like I grow mine here. But the store-bought will never be as good as the ones you grow in your own garden. Now, come see what I have for you."

We walked over to a pot that sat next to the screen door leading into the kitchen.

"I want you to take this home."

"What is it?" I asked as she lifted the pot. There was only dirt with a very small stem growing up out of it.

"It's a tomato plant. I just bought it a few days ago."

"Just like the ones over there?"

"Exactly like the ones over there. And if you take care of it you'll have your own tomatoes that you can eat."

I almost danced at the prospect. No more waiting on my mother to prepare dinner. I dreamed of bags of tomatoes stashed away beneath my bed. Pillowcases lumpy with them stacked in the back of my closet.

"Now, remember to give it water every day and make sure you put it somewhere where it can get lots of sun."

I was so overwhelmed that I forgot to thank her. Instead I sprinted through the yard, barreling through the short hedge lining the property and into the house where my mother was at the sink cleaning the dishes.

"I hope you didn't bother that poor woman too much Miles," she said hearing me stampede into the room. "She must be absolutely beside herself with grief. Fifty two years they'd been married. Then out of the blue," she shook her head to herself. "Such a shame."

"I didn't, but look, look," I said holding the planter up. "Mrs. Bowlan gave me a tomato plant. We don't have to go to the store anymore. She showed me how to grow my own food."

"Oh, my. How lovely," she replied bending over to admire it. "She certainly didn't need to do that. I hope you thanked her."

"I did," I lied.

"Why don't we put it in the back yard so it can get lots of sun."

"But then Dad will eat all of them!"

My mother was one of those people who laughed with her whole body. It was very feminine, but controlled as if she'd been taught somewhere that it was impolite to laugh too hard.

"Oh, my goodness," she said wiping a joyful tear from her eye. "Well then, we'll just have to put it somewhere that he won't notice. I think it'll be safe."

A couple of days later we attended Mr. Bowlan's funeral. Other than ourselves and some distant relatives there was no one else there. Mrs. Bowlan sat next to her weeping family, still and silent, wearing a black dress and perfume I could smell from across the isle. My mother kept whispering to my father how well Mrs. Bowlan was taking everything and how good she looked. He only replied with nods and small grunts.

After the service, I followed my mother to the line that had formed near Mrs. Bowlan. When it was our turn to impart a few sympathetic words, my mother, tears streaming down her face, hugged a dry eyed Mrs. Bowlan.

"Oh, Mary. I'm so sorry. He was such a good man."

"Thank you, dear," Mrs. Bowlan replied.

"Now remember, if you need anything, anything at all, we're just right next door. You don't hesitate to call or come right over."

"I appreciate that, but you don't need to worry about me. Oh, but there is one thing," she said and leaned over to me. "How would you like to help me put a scarecrow up in that garden of mine, young man? Those birds have been giving me trouble lately and besides, I've always wanted a scarecrow."

I nodded my head, knowing it would be rude to say no.

"Good," she said slowly straightening herself.

"We can start after lunch tomorrow."

As planned, the following day after lunch I walked over to help Mrs. Bowlan. It had rained the night before, and since my father had mowed the grass that morning my shoes were heavy with clippings when I reached her doorstep. She answered the door, wearing a smile.

"Hello, dear. Follow me," she said moving through the living room.

"Now, I had all of the materials we need delivered this morning, so…" Her speech stopped and I saw her face twist into a quiet kind of horror as she looked behind me. I turned, half-expecting to see a deranged killer crouching in the doorway, but there was nothing. And then I saw the wet grassy footprints I had shed on the carpet. When I turned around to apologize she was no longer there. A second later she came racing from the kitchen carrying a spray bottle and a rag. She dropped to her knees and began to furiously spray and scrub at the green footprints. As she scrubbed she kept repeating to herself in a low voice "no, no no no, no, he wouldn't allow it. Oh, no no."

"I'm sorry," I said quietly. Surely this would be reported to my mother, and I would have to return the tomato plant. The small sound of my voice seemed to bring her out of a trance. She stopped scrubbing and looked up at me lacking all traces of the fire that had consumed her a moment ago.

"That's alright, dear," she said straightening herself from her prostrated position. "It doesn't matter anymore. Why don't you go on out back and wait for me there. I'll be out in a minute." I nodded my head and crept carefully the rest of the way, shedding as little dirt as possible so as not to bring on any more trouble. When I got out back I headed over to the vegetable garden. A bale of hay, a thin post and some rope sat in the corner of the yard. It reminded me of a fair that I'd been to, in the fall, with pumpkin tosses and hay rides. There were scarecrows posted everywhere, eerily grinning down at you from their crosses.

Mrs. Bowlan came through the back door with an armload of clothes. Her movements were slow but steady and she wore an almost apologetic grin.

"Ok, now," she said as she approached me. "I see you've found the materials. I've brought some old work clothes of Mr. Bowlan's. Here, you take the pants, I'll take the shirt, just grab some hay and start stuffing."

I sat next to the tomato plants stuffing an old pair of tan slacks. Occasionally I would look over at Mrs. Bowlan to be sure I was stuffing properly, and a little too often I would get distracted by the rows of vegetables growing next to me. But if Mrs. Bowlan noticed my lapses in labor, she never said anything.

"There we go," she said holding up the stuffed blue and green flannel shirt. "Nice and tight, like that," as she patted the chest. Now, while you finish the pants I'm going to go inside and see if I can't find something to use for a head." She rose slowly from her chair and eventually disappeared into the house. I began grabbing as much hay as my small hands could hold and stuffed wildly so that when she came back she would be impressed.

When she returned about ten minutes later I had just barely reached my goal. I stood up holding the stuffed slacks next to me like a trophy. They were just as tall as I was and I'm sure if my mother had been there she would have made me stand next to them until she could get a picture.

"Aren't those lovely," Mrs. Bowlan said as she approached. "Alright, I've found some cloth we can use for a head. I'll do that while you take that rope right over there, stuff the shirt into the pants and then tie them together. Just like you're tying a shoelace."

I followed her instructions, awkwardly trying to maneuver two halves of a body that was twice as big as mine. After she had stuffed the head, we tucked it into the shirt collar, tied a rope around that, and then hung the body on the wooden post.

"Oh, gracious," she said heading back inside. "I almost forgot. Wait right there." She returned a minute later with a black sharpie. "The poor thing doesn't even have a face. How can he be expected to scare off anything without a face?"

After sketching a cartoonish expression on the tan cloth we stood back and looked the whole thing over.

"What do you think?" she asked.

"He should be scary," I replied.

"You think so?"

"Yea," I said, doing my best monster face.

"Oh, my goodness, you're right. Let's see here," she pointed the eyebrows downward and added a frown. "Yes. I think that'll do. The crows won't like that one bit. Now how are we going to stand him up?"

I had no response but to shrug and smile.

"Well, there's a ladder in the garage. See if you can bring it around back, and there should be a hammer on one of the work benches in there too. Bring that as well. The button to open the garage is right next to the door as you go in."

I ran through the house and into the garage. The button was just enough out of reach that I had to jump and swat at it a few times to activate it. Finally the motor clicked on with a deep buzzing sound as the garage opened, filling with sunlight. The light revealed two work benches with all kinds of tools meticulously arranged and preserved lining the walls above both of them. There wasn't a spot of rust or corrosion on any of them. They looked just as pristine as if they'd been bought that day.

I saw the ladder lying on its side against the back wall and dragged it out to the driveway before remembering the hammer. I found it lying on one of the work benches just as she said it would be. Having no place else to put it I stuck it under my belt, then managed to drag the ladder to the back gate. Mrs. Bowlan helped me carry it the rest of the way over to the garden. She stepped gently between the rows of vegetables to hold up the stake with the scarecrow while I climbed the ladder and hammered it in with as much force as my arms could muster.

Once it was firmly planted in the soil we both took a step back and admired it.

"I think it's still missing something," she said. "Wait here." She returned with a dirty baseball cap with the mesh in the back and the name of some company printed on the front. "Why don't you climb up there and see how that fits." I scurried up the ladder and placed the cap on the cloth scalp. It slid right on without even having to be adjusted.

"Now, how's that?"

"I don't see any birds," I replied.

"Then it must be working."

A sort of blankness washed over her face as she continued to stand before the scarecrow. I could tell that somehow she wasn't seeing the same thing I saw and I continued to stare with her hoping that whatever it was would reveal itself. But, of course, I saw nothing, only a scarecrow.

"Well," she finally said in a tone that barely trumped a whisper. "I'm feeling a little tired. Why don't you get the ladder put away and meet me in the living room."

I carried it to the garage and leaned it back against the same wall where I'd taken it. After getting the garage to close on the first jump I made my way to the living room. I noticed that there wasn't a single trace of grass left. She'd scrubbed it all completely out.

"Thank you very much for your help," she said handing me five dollars. "You did a wonderful job."

I remembered to thank her this time, then went running through the yard back to my house. The rest of my day was spent reading through a gardening book that my mother had picked up for me at the library. I sat out back, next to my plant, with the book spread wide in my lap, my eyes devouring the pictures of people holding tomatoes the size of baseballs.

Before bed that night I went out to check one last time for any signs of growth. As I squatted down next to the pot I heard a low voice coming from nearby. I followed it over to the wooden fence that separated our yard from Mrs. Bowlan's. Being too short to see over I crouched down and peered through the slots between the boards. I saw Mrs. Bowlan standing in front of the scarecrow. Her right hand clutched the sleeve of the flannel shirt, and she was up on her toes speaking softly to it. Her body seemed to be straining to stretch itself far enough for her lips to reach where an ear would be, if it'd had one. A pair of large square glasses, that I didn't remember us putting on, now rested on the scarecrow's face. I wasn't sure what to make of the scene, but I had one of those strange feelings that it wasn't something I was supposed to be seeing. As I ducked back inside I decided against telling anyone. Surely I'd be scolded for spying.

When I awoke the next morning I went out back, as I had every morning, to see if my plant had grown a miraculous six feet over night with tomatoes the size of basketballs hanging from it. Of course it wasn't so. Before I shuffled back inside for breakfast the mysteries from the past night called.

I squinted through the slots and saw no scarecrow where we had erected one the previous day. It lay a few feet from the garden in a puddle of its own straw. The baseball cap had rolled to the side and a garden hoe was buried deep in the tan cloth where the glasses had rested.

# COMIC BOOKS AS AN EDITORIAL MEDIUM
Stephen Moles
Volume 2, Issue I

I flip through the marked-up pages, pretending to be looking for something, when really I'm formulating my critique. "I don't lose track of your characters," I say, "but the doctor and the teen both seem auxiliary to the story. Have you thought of folding them into one character?" Quizzically, she stares at me, like someone who has just had gravity explained to them for the first time. But then another emotion slowly takes over her face; inspiration. I can see fireworks behind her eyes.

This suggestion seems rather routine to me. It's because I've read characters whittled down and repurposed many times. I've flipped through brightly colored pages where Lex Luthor has been mad scientist, goof ball in green armor, corrupt business man, or President of the United States, depending on the writer's whim. Comic books[1] have spilled a thousand variations into my subconscious and their plurality bubbles up when I'm editing, allowing me a malleability I might not have otherwise.

Comic books are an editorially intense medium. The main reason for this is that there is a great deal of limitations to the form. There is a restriction on physical format, as most monthly comic books are set at strict page count.[2] The second restriction is that stories exist within a shared continuity. Each publisher's stories,

---

1 When I'm discussing "comic books" within the confines of this essay, I'm referring to mainstream superhero comic books produced by the two biggest American publishers: Marvel Comics and DC comics. This is not to say that comics produced by other publishers or in other genres are somehow inferior to the spandex-clad variety, but writing the term "mainstream superhero comics produced by Marvel and DC" over and over is cumbersome.

2 For years, the standard American comic was 22 pages of story (a total of 36 pages including advertisements and letter columns). However, in the recent economic downturn, both Marvel and DC have reduced their page count to 20 pages to keep their books profitable and at the reasonable $2.99 price point.

both Marvel's and DC's, are based in internally consistent fictional universes. Both Spiderman's and the Avengers' stories take place in the same fictional Manhattan, meaning that if a super villain blows up Trump Tower in *The Amazing Spider-Man,* it can't show up intact the next month in *The New Avengers.* Unless the companies want to shatter the delicate realities they've created and stoke the ire of some fanboys. As both publishers have 40+ titles that come out in their respective shared universes each month, a great deal of editorial oversight is required to maintain a semblance of continuity. The final limitation is one that is common to all types of genre fiction: tropes. Whenever a reader comes to a piece of genre fiction, they bring along with them a set of expectations. With superhero comic books some of the expectations are alliterative names, colorful costumes, super powers, robots, flamboyant villains, secret headquarters etc. Part of the pleasure of reading genre fiction is how these tropes are dealt with–if they are indulged, discarded, bent, reified or subverted. While all of these restrictions can be controlled by the writer of a comic book, ultimately it is the editor who has final say in these matters.

It can be argued that there are other types of periodicals, like magazines and newspapers, which also have a great deal of editorial control of content. But the difference between those types of periodicals and comic books is how editorial affects content. For example, most fashion magazines are a vehicle to present clothing. The clothing exists independent of the magazine. It is the raw material that is mediated editorially. In comic books, the raw material (the characters, the concepts, and the form) does not exist outside the medium it is presented in. Thus the editor has a much more direct and obvious contribution to the work.

Comic books also traffic in a trait closely related to editing, what I term "plurality." Comic books have been around for well over seventy years (the original *Action Comics #1* came out in 1938). They have existed through wars, hippies, disco, Reaganomics and multiple waves of feminism. Some of the characters have passed through the hands of hundreds of creators. They have been rearranged to fit the sensibilities of various eras and many (if not all) of these iterations can be accessed by the average reader.

Probably the best example of this plurality is Batman. Created in 1939 by Bob Kane and Bill Finger, Batman's popularity has been steady for most of his publication history. The central concept of Batman is totemic: a young boy sees his parents killed and so he becomes a dark hero in the hopes that no one will ever suffer the same trauma that he did. This has always been the starting point, but the mythos has been spun out innumerable ways. And almost everyone has internalized a few versions of Batman: the campy Adam West 60s TV show, Frank Miller's *Dark Knight,* gothic bleakness of the Tim Burton films, Bruce Timm's cartoon series of the 90s, the kid friendly version of *Batman: the Brave and the Bold,* and Christopher Nolan's hardboiled urban warrior. There are many versions of Batman competing in the public imagination, yet there isn't a definitive take on Batman. This point is so true that there have been two different Batman cartoons that have employed a *Canterbury Tales*-type device, where a group of children tell stories they've heard of "the Batman." Each child's story is based in a different rendition of Batman through the ages. At the end of story time, the "real" Batman shows up and beats up a villain, typically validating at least part of each of the child's interpretations.

This plurality is even a subject of regular discussion among fans and writers alike. Below is an excerpt from an interview with Grant Morrison about his revamp of *Action Comics* that happened in September.

**Nrama:** Lois and Clark aren't married in this version, and we've heard that Lois even has a boyfriend. The new readers you're targeting may have never been aware of their marriage. But how would you describe their relationship now, in this new comic, and how important a role will it play in the story?

**Morrison:** In *Action [Comics],* the first six issues, they barely know one another. Lois is sort of a girl about town, a rising reporter. And Clark Kent works for the rival newspaper. In my first six issues, he doesn't even work for *The Daily Planet,* but Lois and Jimmy [Olsen] do. And Clark works for *The Daily Star.* So they're kind of rivals. And she doesn't even have the thing about Superman yet. Superman's only just come on the scene. She gave him the name. And she's obviously fascinated by him. But there's a lot more to Lois than that.

What's interesting about this excerpt is that Lois and Clark as married couple, newspaper rivals and complicated romantic entanglement is cited in just a few sentences. The plurality of these characters is brought front and center in these statements and the most iconic of these pluralities (the classic Clark Kent/Lois Lane/Superman love triangle) is even alluded to in question. Comic book news publications are rife with content such as Morrison's interviews.

Plurality, in the editorial sense, is not just being able to see the potential within a piece of text. It is an editor's ability to work towards that potential. It is being able to rearrange chunks of text or change a character to make them better. Plurality is not just understanding that a story can be told a thousand different ways, but actually being able to apply that knowledge in a concrete way.

So as I grew up, devouring comic books on a weekly basis, I was constantly exposed to a plurality of characters and concepts. Pairing that with the constant discussion of form and content that could be found on comic book news blogs made it so that I saw comics (and by extension literature or any type of art) as an infinitely moldable medium. Characters could be imagined and reimagined. While certain interpretations were more effective than others, none were absolute. And it is this creative flexibility that I believe all editors (and writers) would be well advised to learn.

When I edit, I am usually balled up on my couch, scribbling marginalia, deep in another person's world. Sometimes, unfortunately, I hit a point where I'm not sure what to say. I'm left with that vague feeling of dissatisfaction, a feeling similar to taste left behind by a fat-free Fudgesicle. Yet I don't know what needs to be changed. I uncurl from the couch and make a trip to my bookshelf. My vision hops over titles. I have three different versions on Superman's origins on my shelves: *Secret Origin, Man of Steel* and the new *Action Comics.* I'll grab whatever pulls at me that day. As I look at the pictures and read the text, I try not to get lost in the story, but to look at it with an editor's eye, trying to see the choices the writer made and wondering what I can learn from them.

# AMIDST EVIL
Katie Flanagan
Volume I, Issue 3

Ola lay in bed that night listening to her parents argue as she tried to fall asleep. With the duvet wrapped around her, she stared up at the ceiling and tried to convince herself not to listen.

The white plaster of the ceiling was cracked, and every now and then when the upstairs neighbors stepped too hard it would crumble down on her. Tata said there was nothing to be done about it: the apartment was old and that was that. Mama had just said "Father knows best" and closed her mouth, her lips curving in a thin line.

Ola didn't mind the apartment, even if it was old and rained plaster sometimes. She liked the way the wooden floors creaked under her feet, although it made it hard to sneak into the kitchen at night to suck on the sweet pickles. She and her younger brother Piotrek had found that one of the floorboards in her bedroom came off, revealing a small hole just perfect for hiding things. Ola had spent hours trying to decide what to hide in there, finally deciding on 10 zloty and her small stuffed bear from when she was little. She wondered what other people who had lived in the apartment had hidden.

Blinking, Ola's thoughts returned to her parents' voices.

*"Gdzie są moje koszulki? Kiedy je wypierzesz?"*

*"A kiedy będziesz wystarczająco trezwy aby wrocić do pracy?"*

It didn't matter that their voices cut in and out so that she couldn't understand everything they said; all she needed to hear was the anger and she understood the argument.

Ola forced herself to think again of the apartment. She thought it was wonderful, even if Bogna wasn't allowed to visit there. Her friend's mother didn't like that the apartment was on ulica Chlodna, said that there was too much evil left in the Jewish quarter. Instead, Ola had to take the tram up to Zoliborz if she wanted to play with Bogna. No one raised any issue with using the trams even though they had been around before the war too. Ola knew because they were in the movie at the Historical Museum about when Warsaw had been the "Paris of Eastern Europe." That was before the Germans and Russians had invaded and the West had betrayed Poland and given it to Stalin.

Ola didn't mind living in the Jewish quarter. Walking home from the bus station, she and Piotrek would count the holes in the side of the building: the pock marks were spread out at first, but by the time she and Piotrek got to their door, the craters were spattered across the wall in a beautiful design that almost looked like a seashell. But when they'd showed Mama the design, her lips had pulled back into a thin curve and she told them the holes were from bullets and they shouldn't think about them.

The smell of raspberry tea reached Ola's nose and she very nearly got out of bed. She loved having tea with Mama late at night, especially when it was just the two of them alone. But then Tata spoke, and Ola wrapped the duvet even tighter around her.

"*Nie wolno! Nie wolno!*"

She wondered if Piotrek had wandered out of his room for some tea, or if Tata was just scolding Mama like she was a child. His words were slurred and Ola could imagine him reaching after Mama angrily as she tried to clear his glass or put the *wódka* bottle back in the cabinet.

Ola didn't understand why people still referred to it as the Jewish quarter. They didn't really, not when they were giving directions or driving through it. But whenever they found out where Ola lived, their breath would stop and their eyes would widen and they would say, "The Jewish Quarter?"

Ola didn't see the problem with it. After all, it wasn't like there were any Jews left.

Babcia said that she had known some Jews growing up. It was hard to imagine because Ola had never met a Jew. Mama had once pointed out a building that was where they worshipped—a *synagoga*—and explained that Jews didn't believe in Jesus. Ola couldn't understand not believing in Jesus. She wondered if maybe the Jews really did believe but were just afraid to say so.

Mama was Babcia's oldest daughter, so Babcia should have been living with them. But Babcia had refused, saying she couldn't stand to live in a graveyard. Instead she moved in with Ciocia Agnieszka in Konstancin and now they all had to drive half an hour to visit each Sunday. Ola wouldn't have minded because the house in Konstancin had a huge garden and in the summertime they could run around outside, but she didn't like being trapped in the car for so long.

Tata's voice was rising and now it was just him yelling. Ola pictured Mama standing by the sink washing the dishes, or maybe sitting at the kitchen table drinking her tea. She wondered if Mama was trying not to listen to the argument, too.

Babcia had tried to stop them from moving into the apartment in the Jewish quarter in the first place. She said that if Mama had been alive during the war like Babcia had, she would know better than to move into an apartment like that. Mama had replied that it was better than living in one of the *bloki*, the blocs put up by the Communist government. Then she had shown Babcia the large rooms, the windows that let in so much sunlight, the courtyard where Ola and Piotrek could play. And Babcia had just shaken her head. "It's not good to live amidst so much evil."

The argument ended quickly and loudly. Hand against cheekbone. Clattering dishes. Sobs.

Ola closed her eyes to the sounds she was supposed to ignore. Her grandmother's words returned.

"It's not good to live amidst so much evil."

Sometimes Ola wondered whether Babcia meant the apartment, or the people inside it.

# PAPER PALACE
Jami Kali
Volume 2, Issue 2


Maybe today would be fun
if instead of fighting
we fuck
or walk under waterfalls
with heavy hearts
and whisper in each others ears
about eyes and Oms and odds
and fall forever
into a faster failing plan
involving paper palaces
and play-money.

Maybe today would be fun
if we call ourselves seeds
and count flowers in the forest
instead of earth's faults
and find common ground
from which we've both sprung
and lower onto leaves
in surrender
to the Sun.

# THE RED MARBLE
Ekaterina Tikhoniouk
Volume 2, Issue 3

Years afterwards, my mother told me that after the move I had woken up crying every night for almost a month. My anguished sobs made her wish that she hadn't uprooted us to this wet and dreary little country.

My night-time hysterics had started the moment they put me in playschool, and in the last two weeks before September, my parents began to worry about me starting 'real' school. A neighbor declared that my distress was probably because I couldn't understand the language, so they set about pouring as much English into my little brain as it could hold.

But I had no memory of my tears and screams, or the fact that I'd obviously decided to hate my new home—all I can remember of that first month in Ireland, is my first day at school.

And the marbles.

I recall being woken up very early that day and being given a new outfit to wear. True, I'd tried it on in the shop weeks ago, but had forgotten all about it. The knee-length flowy skirt and matching knee-high socks delighted me, but the piece of material that my mother tied around my neck was puzzling. They called it a 'tie', but the word was meaningless to me. My older brother, Sergei, who had been in proper school a whole two years before the move, didn't like the clothes one bit, especially this 'tie', as try as he might, he couldn't put it around his neck properly.

"I don't want to wear it Mama. It's stupid. The whole clothes are stupid. Why can't I wear what I want, just like in my old school?"

"The clothes aren't stupid," she answered wearily from where she was ironing one of my father's shirts. "And it's different here. Besides, you look very grown-up in your uniform."

But my brother wouldn't believe her one bit—he even laughed at me when I danced around our living room, making my pretty new skirt swirl around my knees.

"You know that everyone will be wearing the same as you."

"No they won't!" I cried out. "Mine will be the prettiest skirt in the whole school. Just you see."

But it was as he'd said—droves of children dressed just the same as us. We had lived in a little village not far from the outskirts of Minsk. I had seen our school many times—a small whitewashed building beside a tarmac road, so I wasn't expecting the huge school, the crowd of children and parents. The place scared me.

"Mama." I latched onto her arm.

"Katyenka, come on," she sighed. "It's not so bad, it'll be like an adventure."

I said nothing, only gripped her coat sleeve even harder. Heart pounding, I buried my head in the soft brown material as a nearby group of boys began to look at me curiously.

One of the older boys came over and blabbered something at me. He smiling encouragingly, but all I did was try to hide deeper in the folds of my mother's coat. The boy gave a final shrug and went back to his friends, still talking in that strange way.

My brother had learnt a good deal of this funny language in school already, so he marched right up to these boys and began to make the same funny noises, except slower and sounding even funnier than them. The boys must have understood him though, as they answered back. I crept closer, listening to the gibberish coming from their mouths.

Taking advantage of my curiosity, my mother nudged me forward. "Come on, let's go inside."

The classroom she led me into was frightening, with rows and rows of tables facing a board. I was sat down at one of these by a kind-looking woman.

"He-lo Kathy," she said slowly.

I began telling her that wasn't my name, it was Katia, but she just stared back blankly and patted my hair. I don't recall much of what went on in that class, except that I spent the whole morning fighting back tears—I'd found that, yet again, I couldn't understand anyone and no-one could understand me.

But I do remember my relief when the lovely woman finally herded us all out of the classroom for lunch. But my heart sank when I made it out the classroom door—children were pouring out of nearby rooms and the corridor was filled with people. I managed to catch sight of Sergei in the crush and followed his curly-haired head outside. Once he reached the playground he suddenly stopped and I bumped straight into his back.

He turned. "Oh, it's you. You have to go somewhere else, because I'm going over there." He pointed to a group of boys on our left.

"Can't I come with you?" I wailed in desperation.

"No."

"But why?"

"Because."

"Because what?"

"Because. Boys don't play with girls. Especially with little silly ones like you."

"They do! I bet they do."

"Hah! You don't know anything, you're just four."

"I'm four and a *half*," I huffed. "And I'll be real big when I turn five!"

"Go away," my brother growled and pushed me away.

"No!" I stood my ground as I had nowhere else to go; I didn't want to spend lunch hiding alone in some corner.

Just as my brother was reaching out to push me again, a little blonde girl ran over and began pummeling him with her fists. At first he did nothing, but after recovering from his shock, he lightly pushed her away. That didn't seem to faze her. Instead she began to talk very quickly, occasionally pausing to prod him menacingly in the chest with a scrawny finger. Then she reached out to push him, and Sergei stepped back in alarm. The boys behind him guffawed, and so did I—he was about twice the size of her and she was winning!

Feeling her triumph, she pointed at me a few times, before continuing her lecturing, all the while angrily poking his chest with her finger. Sergei even managed to look a little ashamed.

When she was finished with him, she marched over and

looked me up and down. She had blonde hair tied up in a messy ponytail and eyes the colour of blue sky.

"Hi," she finally announced.

Wide-eyed, I could think of nothing to say. I couldn't understand what this "hi" word meant—Papa had never taught me it. Could she be saying hello? I didn't know what to do—I wanted to say something, but was too ashamed. What if I said something wrong? But then I looked past her and saw the taunting grin on my brother's face, and that decided it.

"He-lo," I did my best. "Haw ar-yoo."

She regarded me in silence. Just as I began to think she hadn't understood, she smiled at me.

"Hello, hello!" She smiled again and I saw that there was a huge gap between her two front teeth.

She said something I didn't understand. She kept saying it and pointing to the other end of the playground. I turned to my brother.

For a second it looked like he was going to help, but then he glanced back to his newfound friends and sneered. "Go away Stupid, you're embarrassing me." He took a threatening step forward.

I didn't move.

"That's my new friend," I pointed at the girl, "and if you push me again, she'll hit you."

"She won't, she's just a little baby like you."

But he didn't go near me again, not in front of her.

Grabbing my hand, she pulled me towards the edge of the playground, where she happily plopped down onto the tarmac. I sat down beside her, stealing glances at this funny little girl.

She suddenly proffered her hand, pointing to herself with the other. "Oleveeiah."

"Oh-leev-ee?" I tried.

"Oh-lee-veeee-*ahhh*!" she hollered, but then grinned, deciding that Oleevee would do.

She pointed questioningly at me.

"Kat-ee-ah."

She pointed to herself and lifted up five fingers. I lifted up four fingers, then wiggled my thumb, to show that I was four and *a half*.

Introductions being over with, she quickly looked around to see if anyone was watching us, and slyly produced a handful of coloured glass balls from her pocket. She held up the biggest one, a pretty red one with swirls of orange and yellow.

"Maaaar-ble," she told me and pointed at me until I said it after her a few times. Satisfied with her student, she sat back and rolled a few of the marbles towards me. I reached for the pretty red one but she quickly grabbed it away, with a shake of her disheveled head. Only Oleevee was allowed to play with that one.

Soon she bored of the marbles, and pulled me off towards a different side of the yard, where there were a few slides and a jungle-gym. I was having great fun until the incident on the jungle gym.

As I was swinging around one of the bars, I bumped into her, knocking the little girl right off her feet. She went down with a yowl, but quickly picked herself up. Eyes watering, she held up a bleeding hand.

"Isvini, isvini!" I cried. *Sorry, sorry!*, but she wouldn't listen.

She ran away from me, trailing bright red droplets across the ground. I sat on the jungle-gym for a while, and the emptying playground began to turn blurry. I saw Sergei pushing through the boys still lingering around the slide, so I wiped at my eyes. If he saw me crying he'd just call me a baby and laugh. He always laughed.

Instead he grabbed my hand and pulled me towards the school.

"Lunch is over, Doofus."

He left me outside my classroom and hurried off to his. With a shock, I saw Oleevee sitting in the front row—she'd been in my class all along. I plonked down in my seat at the back and spent the rest of the day looking sadly at the back of her head. I had hoped she'd be my friend, but that wouldn't happen now—she was never going to speak to me, ever again.

I was almost in tears when Mama came to get us after school. Oleevee was at the school gate too. She saw me and said something to her mama, and to my fright the woman gestured to my Mama. I tried to pull Mama back, but then the other woman marched over to us, and began to make the funny sounds.

Mama gave her a shy smile, and made those funny noises too. The woman replied slowly and deliberately, like talking to a child.

*But my Mama's not a baby,* I wanted to tell her, but was too scared to even open my mouth.

Meanwhile Oleevee shuffled over to me and thrust something into my hand, still smiling in her gap-toothed way.

I was too scared to open my hand all the bus journey home. Only after running up to my room did I open my fist, to find her prized red marble lying in my palm.

I'd found my first friend.

Of course there was no instant magical change—I still woke up crying during the night, I still cried during school because I couldn't understand what they were saying. But it became easier with Oleevee there. The crying fits began to lessen to every second night, then every third or fourth, until they petered out completely. A two whole months after the move, I finally seemed happy.

Now it is fifteen years later, and I sit contentedly typing this at my desk in Dublin. Every now and then I glance up at the red marble gathering dust on my shelf, and smile at the memory of that blonde-haired, gap-toothed little girl.

# CASUALTIES OF A THREE-DAY, ISLAND-WIDE OUTAGE: PEACHES, ANOREXIA, BORDERS

Catherine E. Bailey
Volume I, Issue 4

december rolls over the island
and we are shredded. talons of wind seize
trees like fistfuls of hair and buckle full power lines,
cutting pine needle gashes in the wet and shining streets—thin
matchsticks of foliage weeping from the womb of an emerald,
detonated sky.

abandoning the spirals of breath that rise in the air of our house,
we pick our way, mittens kissing, over cragged, rueful branches
that grasp our woolen ankles like fairy tale claws.

we tiptoe like doe in unfamiliar wasteland,
seeking out breakfast and visions of moss. eyefuls of yards
made feral by storms tense thrilling veins and cajole laughing spines.

in the distance, the sea churns, its bottomless stomach toppling fish,
while the hip of the sun shifts carelessly under oyster-and-pearl
colored sheets.

at the market, a girl in braids and a green apron
shimmers with rain and pleasant manners,
bestowing bags of frozen fruit—why keep what won't sell?
the gluey orange syrup stains her hands already, mixing with frost
from the cold cut corpses of slowly melting peaches.

you announce the menu—*bloody mary soup!*—and demand

the freshest tomatoes. wrists wrestle paper cornucopias
of red and ready circles and thick and heavy vines
as we wander fallen branches with wiser, knowing feet.

we cook on a camp stove by candlelight
and wash our hair in enormous pots
of warm and silver water,
prowling the floorboards like mermaids wearing large, ill-fitting
shirts.
coral fingers tussle tresses and stir the steaming brew.

the garnet liquid bubbles, purring of oregano
and I am startled to find
for the first time in years
the feeling of hunger unabated by shame—
the ascetic corset abruptly unlatched.

at night you are all silhouette, and my curved
thoughts sway in the U beneath your ribs.
quietly we sleep, borderless and outside of time.
beyond the windows the sea rages on,
grey and indiscernible from sky.

# CONTRIBUTORS

ANDREW ARSLAN currently lives in New York and is a graduate of John Jay College. His work has also appeared in the Bold Strokes Books anthology, *OMGQUEER: Short Stories by Queer Youth*. You can follow him on Twitter: @AndrewArslan.

LANA HECHTMAN AYERS is a poetry publisher, writing workshop facilitator, manuscript organizer, and aspiring novelist. Her fifth collection of poems, *A New Red*, a contemporary retelling of Red Riding Hood, was published by Pecan Grove Press in 2010. Originally from New York, Lana lives on a peninsula in the Puget Sound with her husband and several monochromatic animals.

JADE LEONE BLACKWATER writes poems to shout at the ocean, essays to honor trees, and feature stories that promote local businesses. Read her prose and poetry in *Wild River Review, Line Zero, The Monongahela Review*, and others. Jade prefers garden mud and forest duff over polite society. brainripples.com.

JENNIFER BRENNOCK is currently at work on two books: the novel *Not Jewish*, forthcoming this year from Pink Fish Press, and a memoir about infertility, adoption, and *The Velveteen Rabbit*. More of her nonfiction can be found in *Shark Reef, The Pitkin Review*, and the anthology *Becoming: What Makes a Woman*.

ELYSE BROWNELL was born and raised on the shores of Lake Superior in Marquette, MI. She is an MFA candidate at the Jack Kerouac School of Disembodied Poetics in Boulder, CO. Elyse is a writer, performer, and curates the monthly performance series, Bouldering Poets. Her work has been published in several journals including *Bombay Gin, Monkey Puzzle Press, Emergency Index, Semicolon, Line Zero, Hoarse*, and her self-published chapbook *Floating Away* was released in 2012. Elyse also received the 2011 Summery Poetry Award for *Line Zero*. Her current project involves sinkholes, memory, and lost postcards.

KEN DAVIS is a regular, occasional contributor to *Line Zero* and is a fan of unconventional writing. His projects lie in offbeat, spiritual fiction. He has completed three novels which, after publication, he intends to retire on; he just needs one good movie deal. Until then, he continues to work on his craft which includes two more novels that are works in progress and one really great idea for a western. For more of his short stories and essays, check out his website, evolvingwriter.com

JIM DAVIS is a graduate of Knox College and an MFA candidate at Northwestern University. Jim lives, writes, and paints in Chicago, where he

# CONTRIBUTORS

edits the *North Chicago Review*. His work has appeared in *Seneca Review*, *Blue Mesa Review*, *Adroit Journal*, *Poetry Quarterly*, *Whitefish Review*, *The Café Review*, and *Contemporary American Voices*, in addition to winning the *Line Zero* Poetry Contest, *Eye on Life* Poetry Prize, multiple Editor's Choice awards, and a recent nomination for the of the Net Anthology. jimdavispoetry.com.

OLINE EATON blogs about celebrities at findingjackie.com. She lives in London and still does not know what to do with her arms when dancing.

JAMES FOWLER teaches literature at the University of Central Arkansas. His stories have recently appeared in *Best Indie Lit New England* and *Forge*. He has stories forthcoming in *Cave Region Review* and *Elder Mountain*.

JASON FRATICELLI currently lives in Marshall, CA where he works in a boatyard full time, a restaurant part time, and attempts to write in between.

JAMES R. GAPINSKI is an MFA candidate at Goddard College, he teaches short story writing at Mt. Hood Community College, and he's the Managing Editor of *The Conium Review*. James lives in Portland, Oregon with his partner and the standard hermit's assortment of books, video games, and cats.

JOHN GREY is an Australian born poet. Recently published in *International Poetry Review*, *Chrysalis* and the science fiction anthology, *Futuredaze* with work upcoming in Potomac Review, Sanskrit and Fox Cry Review.

SHEILA HAGEMAN is a multi-tasking wife and mother of three who blogs for The Huffington Post. Her memoir, *Stripping Down*, February 2012, from Pink Fish Press, is a meditation on womanhood and body image. Her Decision-Making Guide and Self-Discovery Journal, *THE POLE POSITION: Is Stripping for You? (And How to Stay Healthy Doing It)*, Every Day Create, December 2011, helps women further value their own identities through their quest to understand their motivations. She received her MFA in Creative Writing from Hunter College, CUNY, where she also graduated as valedictorian with her BA in English. She is a Yoga instructor and teaches at Housatonic Community College and University of Bridgeport. Sheila has appeared on numerous radio and TV shows including ABC News, NBC News and Anderson Cooper. To learn more about Sheila and everything she does, please visit SheilaHageman.com or StrippingDown.com.

CHARITY HESTEAD is a writer, blogger, and vintage lover from Port Orchard, WA. She currently lives in Bellingham, WA where she received a Creative Writing degree from Western Washington University, but will

# CONTRIBUTORS

soon drift down to California to dedicate her days to writing once again. She loves Kurt Vonnegut, breakfast, poetry, the Pacific Northwest, street style, and messy hair.

ZACH HIVELY is an Albuquerque native who now lives up the road in Durango, Colorado. His fiction has appeared in *Conceptions Southwest* and *A Thoroughly Good Blue*, and he contributes environmental journalism to *New Mexico Mercury*. He's also a microbeer blogger, freelance editor, occasional scholar, and teacher. For more, please visit znhively.blogspot.com or tweet him @ZachHively.

CALEB KRAUSE is a mental health therapist for children, teens, and adults in Tyler, Texas. In his spare time he writes short stories and poetry with a focus on abstract, avant-garde, and surreal styling.

SONIA LYRIS writes fiction, non-fiction, and the occasional shopping list. She lives in the Pacific Northwest in a long-term relationship with relentless rain, stunning sun-breaks, and glittering mountain ranges. lyris.org.

ADRIAN R. MAGNUSON lives on Whidbey Island, Washington with his partner, Sarah, who shares his love of writing, reading and bird watching. Adrian graduated from the University of Washington with a focus on creative writing. He is a full time writer and an active member of the Whidbey Island Writers Association and Pacific Northwest Writers Association.

SARAH LUCILLE MARCHANT is a Missouri resident and university student, studying journalism, literature, and public relations. Her writing has been published numerous places online and in print, and her first poetry chapbook entitled *spilled, refilled* was released by Walleyed Press in 2012. She intends to write with a richness of emotion and to paint a clear picture of what it means to be human.

SARAH MARTINEZ is the author of *Sex and Death in the American Novel*, which has been nominated for the Washington Book Award. She is currently editing for Booktrope and previously served as Senior Editor for Pink Fish Press. Sarah began her career as Editorial Assistant for the literary agent Andrea Hurst. Visit her website at mywildskies.com

STEPHEN MOLES is a writer based in Brooklyn and holds an MFA in Creative Writing from Columbia University. His fiction can be seen regularly in Contributor Magazine.

LANCE NIZAMI has no formal training in the Arts. He is active in the world's most competitive profession, yet without an institutional appointment or

# CONTRIBUTORS

income. He started writing poetry during a long airplane flight in 2010, and has written much since then in-flight. As of 26 April 2013, he had 93 poems in print or in press, most recently in *Calliope, Owen Wister Review, Up the River,* and *More Said Than Done.*

MARC POLONSKY, author of *The Poetry Reader's Toolkit* (Glencoe/McGraw-Hill), is a writer, editor, and educator in Camp Meeker, CA. His essays and interviews have appeared in *The Sun* magazine, the *Huffington Post,* the *North Bay Bohemian,* the *East Bay Express,* the *East Bay Monthly,* and the *Berkeley Daily Planet.* An English literature and composition teacher for 12 years at Berkeley City College (formerly Vista College), Marc now freelances full-time, writing and ghostwriting from his home office in the Sonoma County redwoods. More of Marc's work can be found on his website, marcwordsmith.com.

EKATERINA TIKHONIOUK is originally from Belarus but has lived in Ireland for 19 years and studies architecture in Dublin. In her free time she belly-dances and writes science articles about genetics, zombies, serial killers, hypnosis, and is in the process of writing her second novel.

JOHN J. WALSH IV is a writer, poet, and practicing believer in the philosophies of Ray Bradbury. He loves the sea, siren muses, and tentacled beasts of the deep, and often finds his stories in the prism lens of a lighthouse. He resides in Los Angeles with his wife. johnjwalshiv.com.

MICHAEL DYLAN WELCH's poetry, essays, and book reviews have appeared in hundreds of journals and anthologies in more than fifteen different languages. He is vice president of the Haiku Society of America, director of the Haiku North America conference, cofounder of the American Haiku Archives, and founder and first president of the Tanka Society of America. Michael has served as editor of Cascade, Tundra, and Woodnotes, and in 2012, a poem from one of his books of translations from the Japanese was printed on 150,000,000 United States postage stamps. His websites are graceguts.com and nahaiwrimo.com, the latter of which is for National Haiku Writing Month, which he founded in 2010. Michael lives in Sammamish, Washington.

ROBERT WEXELBLATT is professor of humanities at Boston University's College of General Studies. He has published essays, stories, and poems in a wide variety of journals, two story collections, *Life in the Temperate Zone* and *The Decline of Our Neighborhood,* a book of essays, *Professors at Play*; his novel, *Zublinka Among Women,* won the Indie Book Awards First Prize for Fiction. His most recent book is a short novel, *Losses.*

ANNA WOOD lives and writes in Istanbul.

PINK FISH PRESS PUBLISHES INDEPENDENT LITERARY **ART.**
WE'RE YOUR PARTNER, CHEERLEADER AND CONFIDANT.
**WE LOVE YOUR WORK AS MUCH AS YOU DO.**
# WE READ EVERYTHING.
**WE ACHIEVE GOALS THROUGH NETWORKING, KNOWLEDGE AND TENACITY.**
AS A PINK FISH PRESS AUTHOR, YOU REPRESENT THE
DIVERGENT NATURE OF EVOLVING LITERATURE WITH
TALENTED, UNIQUE VOICES, STORIES AND CHARACTERS.

**YOU DO NOT GIVE UP; YOU REWRITE, PERFECT, SUBMIT.** WHEN FACED WITH REJECTION YOU REALIZE THAT THE WORST ANSWER YOU CAN HEAR IS NO—WHICH IS ONLY FUEL TO **REFINE AND TRY AGAIN.** YOU MEASURE SUCCESS IN THE NUMBER OF LIVES YOUR WORK TOUCHES AND IMPACTS, NOT IN DOLLARS, REVIEWS OR NOTORIETY.

YOU NEVER STOP LEARNING AND CONSTANTLY CHALLENGE
YOURSELF. YOU PRACTICE, STUDY AND SHARPEN YOUR **ART.**
YOU TELL YOUR STORIES WITH NAKED HONESTY AND WITHOUT APOLOGY.
YOU IMMERSE YOUR STORIES IN LANGUAGE
**SO VISCERAL THAT YOUR READERS**
# DROWN IN IT.
**WE** RECOGNIZE WRITING IS AN **ART.**
**OUR** BOOKS **BEND GENRE** AND **TWIST PERCEPTION.**

EVERY BOOK HAS A DESTINY.
**FIND AND DEFINE YOURS.**
THE PINK FISH PRESS . COM

www.ingramcontent.com/pod-product-compliance
Lightning Source LLC
Chambersburg PA
CBHW020631250626
47154CB00008B/2629